CONTENTS

I   The Person..3

II   Sensation...7

III   Emotion...7

IV   Mentality...9
      A.   Judgement.......................................10
      B.   Inductive Inference.............................13
      C.   Formal Logic....................................14
      D.   Dialectics......................................30
      E.   Laws Of Dialectics..............................32

V   RATIONAL LAWS..37

VI   WILL...47

VII   SELF REALISATION

      i   Introduction...................................49
      ii   General Aspects................................53
      iii   A Philosophy For Living........................60
      iv   Therapeutic Autopsychology
            (a) Psychoanalysis And Self Hypnotism..........63
            (b) Behaviour Modification.....................70
            (c) Meditation.................................74
      v   Consciousness And Mind Control.................78
      vi   Japam..81
      vii   Self Mastery...................................83

ii

VIII   ANTHROPOSOPHY

Human Nature.....................................86
The Love Relationship............................90
General Aspects Of Human Nature.................93
Aspects Of the Person..........................102
Psychological Self Rule........................104
Collective Behaviour...........................109
Sources Of Happiness...........................110
Pain And Pleasure..............................118
ONESELF..119
Problems Of Life...............................121
Pragmatic Guidelines...........................128

IX   The Fundamental Questions Of Philosophy.......135

X   Further Philosophical Aspects.................154

XI   The Absolute..................................160

XII   The ONE.......................................163

XIII The WAY.......................................165

XIV   SPIRITUAL IDEOLOGY............................169

XV   The Nine Great Happinesses....................170

PSYCHOLOGICAL SURVIVAL

BY

KEVIN ANTHONY CHEEVERS

Copyright © 2010 Kevin Anthony Cheevers

ISBN: 978-1-906027-56-8

Printed and bound in Ireland by eprint limited
www.eprint.ie

INTRODUCTION.

The most important lesson to be learned from the study of Psychology is that the Human Person is only partly rational. Nor is reason the highest faculty of Mind. The human being is a particular and individual integration of sensory and mental consciousness overshadowed by their individual subconscious and the collective subconscious of Humanity as a whole. The individual is a Soul, An Ego or Self which is unique and distinct from everyone else. We all have an identity or Ego or "I" which Wills, Thinks and Feels and is the focus of sensation through the senses.

Society came into existence as necessary for the survival of every individual and the satisfaction of bio-social and material needs. The pre-condition for the continuance of society and the possibility of it fulfilling it's original function to any degree is social co-operation between Human Beings. Competition is also endemic in society in relation to individual need to satisfy psychological, bio-social and material requirements for happiness. A balance between competition and co-operation is essential for any society not to fail to endure or survive.

Modern 'class society' produces conflict relating to class appropriation of wealth, power and priviliege. There is consequent individual alienation of a psychological and social character and anomie. The modern individual is 'alone' in society where they are not part of the 'nuclear family' or the 'extended family' and such individuals and many people in general experience a serious frustration of their bio-social, material and psychological needs.

Social and economic conditions tend not only to frustrate human needs, but to pervert them and substitute artificial for authentic needs which cannot find satisfaction. Society in fact is seen to be an apparent conspiracy against Human Nature and the individual in particular is exploited, eschewed and debased by the mass society.

This book is an attempt to address the problem of survival with happiness and sanity in our society. Religion is being seen by an increasing number of people to be irrelevant to this problem in the modern world for it has its origins in the distant past and the intellectual childhood of Man.

This book is unashamedly a simple survival kit for those who have not any faith in the existence of a Creator or the "Good God" and is a philosophically psychological solution which has evolved with the authors personal survival in dire circumstances and his "conquest of happiness".

NO SACRIFICE OF THE REASON.

NO SURRENDER OF THE WILL.

NO SUBMISSION OF THE BODY.

Do not be ruled by feelings of Altruism or Natural Affection and Generosity; Be ruled by Rationality in dealings with people.

Don't be "carried away" by feelings of empathy or sympathy.

I. THE PERSON.

The individual has to everyone else an appearance, expression and attitude; character structure and personality.

The appearance of the person is essentially related to their ultimate nature. The qualities of expression and the facial features of the individual rarely belie their true make-up as humans. Blue eyes are as much an inherited characteristic as intelligence or moral sense. Individuals look like what they are essentially. Appearance is the manifestation of Essence.

There are two aspects to expression. The first "signalling system" and the second "signalling system". The first "signalling system" is facial expression, gesture and body language as well as touch. The first "signalling system" comprises all non-verbal communicaiton between humans distinct from what may be described as "sixth sense", extra-sensory perception or telepathy, if such things can actually be verified.

The second "signalling system" separates Humanity from the rest of the animal world and is articulate verbal communication or speech. Speech is intrinsically linked with the mental development of Man as is the capacity of Man as a toolmaker and worker. It is in speech and labour activity that all intellect and Humanity or Civilisaiton find their origin.

Attitude is physical and emotional as well as mental predisposition resulting from conditioning, accumulated experience and mental reflection. It is inseparable from expression whether verbal or non-verbal.

Character structure is an integration of attitude and general social behaviour rooted in the nature, type and degree of satisfaction of the individuals bio-social and psychological needs.

Personality is the structure of the individuals mentality, emotional make-up and sensory equipment as results from genotype and social being. Social being determines social consciousness and environment is ultimately decisive in the degree of psychological and social development of the individual.

Apperception is the final or ultimate awareness by the individual of themselves. It is consciousness aware of itself. It is the Ego or Self distinguishing between one's "Self Image", one's "Self Ideal" and one's "Actual Self". It is the individual Ego aware of it's own existence. "I am, who am".

Noumenon is the ultimate Whole and total self or Ego which is a unity of our sensory and mental consciousness and our subconscious. It is beyond our full knowledge and comprehension. If we were to know and understand ourselves fully, we would have to rise above that which we are; an obvious impossibility. Though we cannot thus know or understand ourselves fully we can be and are at all times totally ourselves. Be yourself and act unselfconsciously.

The individual is a component of the mass Humanity. Their consciousness is part of the total consciousness of Humanity and their individual subconscious integrated in the collective subconscious of Man. The Will of the individual, a component of their Ego, is part of the collective and general Will of Humanity and ultimately in tune with a Universal Will intrinsic to the existence of Human Life and Consciousness.

The Ego is the centre and focus of a Unity of conscious and subconscious mind. It is that which when thinking "I" or "I am" both proves and verifies it's own existence, or when thoughtless is a focus of sensation and feeling verifying it's existence. One is one's Ego or Self. Ego is Soul.

ANOMIE.

Anomie is a psychological condition of mind in the individual resultant of certain social conditions.

(1)   The absence of a coherent and consistent morality of conviction, resulting from the absence of an identification with existing social mores.

(2)   The absence of bio-social preconditions for the self realisation and natural fulfilment of individual needs, desires and aspirations.

(3)   The social isolation of the individual or "social atomisation" in society.

(4)   The existence of conflicting "class cultures" and distinctly differing "norms" of social behaviour rooted in social class realities, which are at best distortions of natural human behaviour.

(5)   The failure to attain to authentic love relationships with the opposite sex.

(6)   The failure to acquire and hold authentic friends of one's own sex.

(7)   The breakdown of natural perception and spontaneous unselfconscious rationality.

(8)   Lack of faith in Humanity, oneself and any divine power of benevolence or providence.

(9)   Religious and ideological pluralism in society; distinct from adherence to a unitary and unifying world outlook.

(10)   Racial or ethnic antagonism and religious sectarianism.

ALIENATION.

Alienation, is a material social and economic reality as well as psychological condition of the individual

The worker is naturally alienated from the product of their labour which sells at a higher price than the worker earns for its production.

Consumption of the Capitalist is at the expense of the worker who produces all material wealth.

Class and social alienation result from the separation of the worker from the wealth they produce.

Alienation is a consequence of social poverty in opposition to social luxury.

Alienation is also a consequence of ideological, political and social antipathy to the establishment of any society.

Doubt and uncertainty generate anxiety.

Anomie generates despair and hopelessness.

Alienation generates fearfulness and cynicism.

II.   SENSATION.

Sensation is the impression made by objectively existing reality on our Ego through the senses. It is distinct from mental consciousness or thought. Mental consciousness is a derivative of sensory awareness; which forms the basis of existence of thought consciousness and from which our mentality is derivative. "There is not in the mind, what was not first in the senses".

The senses comprise sight, hearing, touch, taste, smell, proprioception. We also have a "time sense" or consciousness of existing or of our own consciousness while conscious; distinct from apperception. We also have an awareness which many people describe as their "sixth sense".

Some people claim to have extra sensory perception and awareness; distinct from thought consciousness.

III.   EMOTION.

Emotion is a unity of mental and sensory consciousness. It is in the body and the mind together. All thought is charged with emotion and all emotion is experienced in the mind and body at once.

The cardinal emotions are:-

    Love and Hate   - Vanity and Humility

    Fear and Anger   - Envy and Jealousy

                Greed.

The emotions are as essential to our survival as our thinking as they are the necessary connection between thought or mentality and physical action.

The emotions have a 'logic' of their own equipping us with survival ability. They are neither "good" nor "evil". They can and do usurp our reason and will at times and they can be very dangerous to ourselves or others when this occurs.

Love is to creation and harmony as Hate is to destruction and discord. Humility deprives us of self respect and confidence whereas Vanity makes us over-confident and selfish. Pride, or "amour propre" is midway between these extremes and is conducive to confidence, poise and effectiveness in society and work.

Fear is to flight as Anger is to Fight.

Envy motivates us to competition. Jealousy motivates us to possession and covetousness.

Greed is the essential of most serious problems of economic justice and material wealth and poverty. It is intrinsic, with all emotions; to the questions of Morality and Politics.

Love and Hate - Vanity and Humility - Fear and Anger; are all pairs of emotional opposites, they can pass one into the other and intermediate states can exist.

V.   RATIONAL LAWS.

1.   MENTAL IMAGES and IDEAS activate the person.

2.   MENTAL IMAGES and IDEAS generate EMOTIONS and corresponding ATTITUDES.

3.   Actions tend to generate related EMOTIONS, ATTITUDES and IMAGES.

4.   EMOTIONS and ATTITUDES tend to awaken and intensify corresponding MENTAL IMAGES and EMOTIONS.

5.   Resolutions of THOUGHT process result in resolutions of EMOTION STRUCTURE.

6.   NEEDS, DRIVES AND DESIRES tend to arouse corresponding IMAGES, IDEAS AND EMOTIONS.

7.   Attention, spontaneous or developed interest, affirmation and repetition all reinforce IMAGES, ATTITUDES and EMOTION on which they are centred.

8.   Repetition results in habituation and renders the execution of tasks easy and automatic.

9.   All our innate NEEDS, DESIRES and DRIVES adopt subconscious strategies for their satisfaction in line with or against conscious volition.

10.   NEEDS, DESIRES AND DRIVES but especially, EMOTIONS demand expression or assertion.

11.   The Association Of Ideas,Facts And Emotions.

The first associations of colour, form, sound, taste and touch come to us from Nature through the senses.

Associations become internally organised in human consciousness in a way that reflects their organisation in Nature.

Sensory images are associated on the basis of their contiguity in experience; their similarity and contrast.

All sensory images have affective components and all derivative mental images retain this emotive element in consciousness.

Mental images and ideas find association on the basis of similiarity , commonality and contrast and the relationship of their affective content in consciousness, as a primary aspect.

We can have association on the basis of judgements of opposites as well as similarity;

E.G.

        Love and Hate
        Beauty and Ugliness
        Hot and Cold
        Dark and Bright

all find association as pairs on the basis of their connection as opposites.

Beauty and ugliness find association through their affective components, with love and hate.

We tend to have a generalised association of all things we love and of all things we hate.

This generalised association operates on all the emotions.

The generalised association of things on the basis of common emotions is Affective Association.

We also tend to have a generalised association of all things that we perceive as similar , disimilar or opposite.

This is Rational Association.

We tend to have a generalised association of things which occur together in space and time.

This is Empirical Association.

Regarding affective association,it can be said that positive and negative feelings, constructive and destructive attitudes,sthenic and asthenic emotions; can all be associated with mental images and ideas of moral right and wrong.

The association of emotion with ideas of right and wrong is called cathechism.

We can be right in two important ways:-

We can be right in our thinking and

We can be right in how we feel about our thought.

The Affective , Empirical and Rational associations of consciousness over periods of personal development all become integrated and related more or less strongly.

These associations, underwritten by the memory form the basis of philosophical capacity.

The other ingredient is logic as intrinsic to human mental processes.

The rational mind is a harmony of thought process and emotional experience,resulting in behavioural stability and the absence of eccentricity or fanaticism.

Rational association is inseparable from the processes of mental judgement and the logical interconnection of ideas.

All events requiring similar types of judgement or logical processes become associated in memory inevitably.

All things of unique or discrete emotional impact find association on the basis of similarity, commonality and disimilarity and are linked with their concrete objects in the external world as experienced over time and retained in the memory.

All things causally related in Nature and Society ultimately find association in the human consciousness and memory; reflecting observed regularities in Nature and Society.

There is correspondence between the senses, in
reality impinging on the Ego through the senses
information received through any one sense does
that coming through any other sense. Sensory images
perceptions form "wholes" and the totality of images remembered
and capable of being remembered form an integrated and
harmonious or coherent and consistent unity reflecting the
unity underlying objective reality.

The images impressed on us through the senses, on being
remembered become mental images rather than sensations and we
can cognise and recognise myriad aspects of reality of which
the senses are the interface and as a consequence of the
capacity to store and recall mental images we are capable of
comparing and analysing them.

Perception is the cognition of the essence and intrinsic
relations of sensuously perceived reality. The cognition and
recognition of Entity in its unity and plurality.

Intuition is the imagination of possible or probable
connections intrinsic to Entity or Hypothetical Reality.
There are four other very important operations of mind which,
inborn and innate to all human beings are:-

(1) Judgement. (2) Inductive Inference. (3) Dialectics.

(4) Deductive Inference.

(5) Other mental functions of paramount importance are those
of numerical reasoning or comparison of natural number
and computation, implicit to which is the recognition of
pattern and form or structure. Mathematics is not
reducible to Formal Logic though it contains it.

(6) The Cognition of Causal Laws is an imperative for all
natural and social science.

JUDGEMENT.

here outline the most important types of Judgement implicit to mental functioning; which constitute the components on which deductive, inductive and dialectical thought operate in order to comprehend reality.

(1) Judgement of Inherence.

Examples:

"Grass is Green"   — Positive.

"Grass is not blue"   — Negative.

"Water is colourless"   — Neutral.

"The brick is red and heavy" — Conjunctive.

"Stone is not grass"   — Infinite.

(2) Judgement of Relation.

Examples:

"Pain results from injury".

"200 is 20 times 10".

"The planets rotate about the Sun".

"The Nile is in Egypt".

(3) Judgement of Subsumption.

Examples:

> "This whale is a mammal"   —   Singular.
>
> "Some creatures are mammals" —   Particular.
>
> "All cars are vehicles"   —   Universal.

(4) Judgement of Necessity.

Examples:

"Men and Women are either equal or different" — Disjunctive.

"Socialism is both necessary and inevitable" — Conjunctive.

> "This flower is a plant"   —   Categorical.
>
> "Unhappiness is misery"   —   Hypothetical.

(5) Judgement of the Idea.

Examples:

"If a marriage lasts its basis is true love" — Problematic.

"A man who does no harm is a moral man"   — Apodeictic.

> "The light is inadequate"   —   Assertoric.

(6) **Judgement-of-Opposition.**

<u>Examples</u>:

"Hot is the opposite of Cold".

"Light is the opposite of Darkness".

"Positive and Negative".

"Right and Wrong".

(7) Other important types of judgement are those of the
     perception of the unity, identity and negation of
     entities. Similarity and. dissimilarity and uniqueness.
     The difference within the equality or identity of
     entities. The judgement that something is equal to,
     greater than or less than another entity.

     The distinction between Quantity and Quality.

     All complex ideas can be reduced to a compound of simple
     irreducible ideas or atomistic concepts interconnected by
     logical form or dialectic unity.

     "That which is distinguishable in the senses or the
      mind is separable in actuality as well as the senses
      and the mind".

B.   **INDUCTIVE INFERENCE.**

I.   If only two events occur and one precedes the other; the one that precedes is a Cause of the one that follows.

II.   If only two events occur, and simultaneously; they are mutually Causal and Conditional.

III.   If two or more situations in which a phenomena occurs have nothing in common save one, that circumstance they share in common is a Cause or an Effect of the phenomena.

IV.   If two circumstances, one in which a phenomena occurs and another in which it does not occur have everything in common save one, the one circumstance in which they differ is a Cause or an Effect of the phenomenon.

V.   If two or more instances of a phenomena have a factor in common and two or more instances in which the phenomena does not occur have nothing in common save the absence of that factor, that factor is a Cause or an Effect of the phenomena.

VI.   Whatever phenomena varies in any manner whatever, whenever another phenomena varies in a particular manner (or vice versa) is either a Cause or an Effect of the variation in the other phenomena.

VII.   If we subtract from any phenomena such part as is known to be the Effect of certain antecedents then the residue is the Effect of the remaining antecedents.

VIII.   If a very large number of instances of a phenomena have a single factor in common, probably all instances have.

FORMAL LOGIC

I   PROPOSITIONS

A proposition is a statement thought to be true or false.   It
is a sentence which affirms or denys something.

(a) PROPOSITIONS ARE OF FOUR KINDS

(1) Affirmative Universal (A) as in
        "All X's are Y's"

(2) Affirmative Particular (I) as in
        "Some X's are Y's"

(3) Negative Universal (E) as in
        "No X's are Y's"

(4) Negative Particular (O) as in
        "Some X's are not Y's"

(b) RELATIONS BETWEEN PROPOSITIONS ARE OF FIVE KINDS

(1) Contradiction exists between (A) and (O) and between (I)
    and (E) propositons.

    If two propositions are contradictory they cannot both be
    true and they cannot both be false. Either one or the
    other must be true.

(2) Contrariety exists between (A) and (E) propositions.   If
    two propositions are contrary they cannot both be true but
    they can both be false.

-15-

(3) Subcontrariety exists between (I) and (O) propositions. If
two propositions are subcontrary they cannot both be false
but they can both be true.

(4) The relationship of (A) propositions to (I) propositions
and of (E) propositions to (O) propositions is
superimplication.

(5) The relationship of (I) propositions to (A) propositions
and of (O) propositions to (E) propositions is
subimplication.

The relationships existing between propositions can be
illustrated by the "Square Of Opposition".

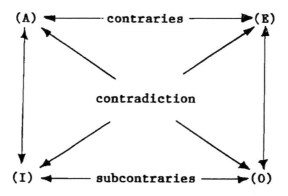

Diagonally opposed propositions are contradictory.
Horizontally opposed propositions are contrary or subcontrary.

EXAMPLES

(1)   Contradiction

    (a)   (A) and (O) Propositions.

        (A)   All X's are Y's.

        (O)   Some X's are not Y's.

    (b)   (I) and (E) Propositions.

        (I)   Some X's are Y's.

        (E)   No X's are Y's.

(2)   Contrariety

    (A) and (E) Propositions.

    (A)   All X's are Y's.

    (E)   No X's are Y's.

(3)   Subcontrary

    (I) and (O) Propositions.

    (I)   Some X's are Y's.

    (O)   Some X's are not Y's

(4)   Superimplication

    (a)   (A) and (I) Propositions.

        (A)   All X's are Y's.

        (I)   Some X's are Y's.

    (b)   (E) and (O) Propositions.

        (E)   No X's are Y's.

        (O)   Some X's are not Y's.

(5)   Subimplication

    (a)   (I) and (A) Propositions.

        (I)   Some X's are Y's.

        (A)   All X's are Y's.

    (b)   (O) and (E) Propositions

        (O)   Some X's are not Y's.

        (E)   No X's are Y's.

(c)   IMMEDIATE INFERENCE

A proposition consists of a Subject and a Predicate connected by a Copula.

E.G.

> "All X's are Y's".
>
> "X" is the Subject.
>
> "Y" is the Predicate.
>
> "are" is the Copula.

The Copula is always some part of the verb "to be".

THERE ARE FOUR KINDS OF IMMEDIATE INFERENCE

(a)   Conversion in which the subject of the proposition is the predicate of the original proposition.

E.G.   "All men are mortals"............Original Proposition.

"Some mortals are men"...........Converted Proposition.

(b)   Inversion in which the subject of the proposition is the contradictory of the subject of the original Proposition.

E.G.   "All men are mortal".............Original Proposition.

       "Immortals are not men"..........Inverted Proposition.

(c)   Obversion in which the predicate of the proposition is
       the contradictory of the predicate of the original
       Proposition.

E.G.   "All men are mortal".............Original Proposition.

       "No men are immortal"............Obverted Proposition.

(d)   Contraposition, in which the subject of the proposition
       is the contradictory of the predicate of the original
       Proposition.

E.G.   "All men are mortal".............Original Proposition.

       "No men are immortal"............Contraposition.

It is essential to note that (0) Propositions cannot be
converted. The Obversion and Contraposition of "All men are
mortal" results in identical statements "No men are immortal".

(d)   DISTRIBUTION OF TERMS IN PROPOSITIONS

(i)   In (A) propositions the subject is distributed and the predicate undistributed.

E.G.

"All X's are Y's".

"X" is distributed because ALL "X" is referred to.

"Y" is undistributed, as all "Y" is not necessarily "X".

(ii)   In (E) propositions the subject is distributed and the predicate undistributed.

E.G.

"No X's are Y's".

"X" is distributed because all "X" is referred to negatively.

"Y" is undistributed as it is excluded from "X".

(iii) In (I) propositions the subject is undistributed and the predicate undistributed also.

E.G.

"Some X's are Y's".

In the case of both "X" and "Y" only some and not all are referred to.

(iv)   In (0) propositions the subject is undistributed but the predicate is distributed.

E.G.

"Some X's are not Y's".

All "X's" are referred to, but all "Y's" are referred to implicitly in a negative sense. So "X" is undistributed and "Y" is distributed.

(e)   THE HYPOTHETICAL PROPOSITION.

The hypothetical proposition takes the form:

"If X then Y".

"If the ground is wet then it has rained".

"If the ground is not wet then is 'has not rained".

Explicitly:

"If X is true than Y is true, otherwise Y is false".

N.B.   The quantity and quality of propositions are defined as:

(i)   Quantity is whether they are universal or particular.

(ii)   Quality is whether they are affirmative or negative.

II. THE SYLLOGISM

(A)   A syllogism is a gathering of three propositions such
      that if I admit the truth of the first and second; I
      must admit the truth of the third, which is termed the
      conclusion.

E.G.

All men are mortal.

I am a man.

(THEREFORE) I shall die.

All wise men are virtuous.

Marx was a wise man.

(THEREFORE) Marx was virtuous.

All tyrants deserve death.

Hitler was a tyrant.

(THEREFORE) Hitler deserved death.

All communists are revolutionaries.

Michael is a communist.

(THEREFORE) Michael is a revolutionary.

If I admit the first two propositions of a syllogism as true and the third logically follows, the syllogism is valid; otherwise it is not.

(B) ANALYSIS OF THE SYLLOGISM

The principles on which syllogistic reasoning depends are:-

(a) If two things agree with a third, then they agree with one another.

(b) If one thing agrees with a third and a second thing does not agree with third; then the first and second things are in disagreement.

(c) If two things disagree with a third then they may either agree or disagree with each other.

(C) AXIOMS OF THE SYLLOGISM.

(1) Axioms of Quality.

(a) At least one premise must be affirmative;
If both premises are negative then no conclusion is possible.

(b) If one premise is negative the conclusion must be negative; otherwise the conclusion must be affirmative.

(2)   Axioms of Distribution.

(a)   The middle term must be distributed in at least one premise.

(b)   A term distributed in the conclusion must be distributed in the corresponding premise.

If a term is undistributed in the conclusion it must be undistributed in the corresponding premise.

(D)   CORROLARIES.

The following corrolaries to the axioms are implied or can be derived.

(1)   At least one premise must be universal.

(2)   Given that one premise is particular, the conclusion must be particular.

(3)   Given that the 'major premise' is particular, the 'minor premise' cannot be negative.

III   RULES FOR VALID SYLLOGISMS.

Rules for valid syllogisms can be reduced to three:-

(1)   There must be only three terms and three propositions.

(2)   The middle term must be distributed in at least one premise.

(3)   No term can be distributed in the conclusion which is not distributed in the corresponding premise and no term undistributed in the conclusion can be distributed in it's corresponding premise.

IF A SYLLOGISM OBEYS THESE THREE RULES IT IS A VALID SYLLOGISM.

The following additional rules are most helpful.

(4)   It is impossible to have two negative premises.

(5)   If there is a negative premise there is a negative conclusion and vice versa.

(6)   No particular conclusion can be entailed in two universal premises.

IV FALLACY

Fallacy is invalid or wrong reasoning. The violation of the rules for valid syllogisms exemplifies logical fallacy.

I NON-LOGICAL FALLACIES

Non-logical fallacies occur when we use ambiguous terms, poorly defined words or propositions that are not clearly understood.

(a) A clear example of fallacious reasoning is the "Argument Against The Person". It consists in saying that because a given person is such and such; say stupid or criminal or uneducated, that their argument is necessarily invalid or wrong. It also has it's obverse in that a person deemed eminent, intelligent or educated is thought to be necessarily correct in their argument.

(b) A clear example of fallacious argument is an appeal to emotion or prejudice. We may temporarily gain the upper hand in a political debate by appealing to the prejudices or sentiments of our audience.

(c) The fallacy of "Irrelevant Conclusion" is essentially setting out to prove something is the case but succeeding in proving something entirely different and irrelevant to the argument.

(d) Circular reasonins is the fallacy of by implication assuming the truth of what it is you are seeking to prove.

(e) "Post Hoc, Ergo Propter Hoc".
This literally means, "Before, therefore because". It is the assumption that because an event preceeded another, it caused it.

(f) Arguing from analogy where the analogy is tenuous or inaccurate leads to erroneous conclusions.

(g) The "Argument from Authority".

EXAMPLE

Einstein was one of the greatest scientists in history. Therefore if he thought the earth was flat, it must be. Or Karl Marx was the founder of modern communism, therefore all his ideas on the subject are true.

The argument from authority is used to prop up academic and ideological conservatism.

II   SEMI-LOGICAL FALLACIES

(a)   Equivocation consists in using the same term in different senses.

E.G. A mouse is a monosyllable.

But a mouse eats cheese.

Therefore monosyllables eat cheese.

"Leaders are the servants of the people and should do as the people wish".

"He who harms another should be punished. A man who communicates disease harms others. Therefore they who pass on contagious diseases should be punished".

"Interference with anothers business is illegal. But to
undersell one's competitors is to interfere with their
business. Therefore to undersell is illegal".

(b) Amphiboly is the fallacy of ambiguous statement.

E.G. "The Greeks the Persians shall subdue".

"The duke yet lives that Henry shall depose".

"Twice 2 and 3 = 7 or 10".

(c) Fallacy of Composition and Division.

This fallacy occurs when the same term is taken
collectively in one case and distributively in another
case.

E.G. "Three and two are five. But three and two are odd and
even. Therefore five is odd and even".

"Each member of the jury can be deceived. Therefore all
may be deceived".

(d) Fallacy of Accent consists in any ambiguity of emphasis.

E.G. "The father said to his sons. 'Saddle the ass' and they
saddled him".

"Thou shalt not bear false witness against thy NEIGHBOUR"
- implying that you may bear false witness against all
others.

(e) Fallacy of Accident.

What is asserted of a substance merely is attributed to it
as to it's conditions and circumstances.

E.G. "What is bought in the market is eaten. But raw meat is
bought in the market. Therefore meat is eaten raw".

DIALECTICS

Dialectics is the human thought process accurately reflecting objective developments in the real world.Dialectic is the ongoing conflict of forces or the 'contradictions' inherent in Nature and manifest as the development of phenomena whether stable or unstable.Dialectic is the thought process reflecting in consciousness such objective phenomena.Dialectics is essentially a unity of inseparable form and content, unlike formal logic where a wide variety of content can be substituted into formal structures and patterns.Dialectics was synonymous with 'Logos' in medieval times when the science of discourse and debate were identified as equivalent.Dialectics was for Heraclitus the contrast of opposites and their apparent identity.Dialectics was for Plato and Aristotle the process of reasoning from probable or assumed premises to arrive at the cognition of higher or more general truths.

Among the most important meanings that have been attributed to dialectics are:-

(1)   The method of refutation by examining logical
      consequences.
(2)   Sophistical reasoning.
(3)   The method of repeated logical analysis of genera into
      species.
(4)   An investigation of extremely abstract concepts by a
      process of reasoning leading from particular cases to
      general hypotheses.
(5)   Logical reasonong or debate employing premises that are
      only probable or are of general acceptance or assent.
(6)   Formal Logic.
(7)   The criticism of the logic of illusion showing the
      contradictions that become explicit when reason seeks to
      go beyond the data of sense experience.

(8)   The logical development of thought that like reality
       moves from thesis to antithesis and then to a synthesis
       of these opposites.

Dialectic was with Hegel essentially the acceptance of the
necessary conformity of thought to reality.The identification
of the 'contradictory' nature of reality and the process of the
resolution of 'contradictions' in the human thought process and
in Nature and Society both.

Dialectics as considered by Dialectical Materialists is the
process of human thought distinct from formal logic,having a
rationality of it's own which describes the objective processes
of Nature and Society as reflected in consciousness.

Dialectical Materialists consider Dialectics and Logic proper
to form an indissoluble unity in both objective reality and
thinking.

OBJECTIVE DIALECTIC IS SYNONYMOUS WITH 'LOGOS'

SUBJECTIVE DIALECTIC IS SYNONYMOUS WITH 'NOUS'.

THE LAWS OF DIALECTICS.

I.   THE UNITY AND CONFLICT OF OPPOSITES.

If we consider the opposite mutually conditional and relatives "hot" and "cold", we can see that "cold" is the absence of "hot" as "hot" is the absence of "cold".

The conflict of opposites is thus absolute; we cannot have both "hot" and "cold" co-existing together in proximity.

If we envisage some intermediate condition between "hot" and "cold" we can describe as being BOTH hot and cold or NEITHER hot nor cold.

This intermediate condition which is exemplified by the equally relevant or irrelevant descriptions of "hot" or "cold" is known as the unity of opposites.

The same hill may be said to slope upwards or downwards at a given point.   Opposites meeting in such intermediate or identical positions are thought to be a unity or identity respectively.   This unity or identity is temporary and relative.

If we mix ice and steam we well get water.   Here the intermediate condition of the opposites "hot" and "cold" are exemplified by a state of existence of matter, namely water, whereas the extremes of "hot" and "cold" are exemplified by the existence of two opposites and hostile states of solid(ice) and gas (steam).

Light and Darkness.

Hot and Cold.

Active and Passive.

Positive and Negative.

Heavy and Light.

Good and Evil.

are all examples of Dialectic Opposites.

Two opposites which do not have an ·intermediate unity or identity in existence are known as "contradictories".

An analogy to 'contradiction' is the phenomena whereby Iodine exists either as a solid or a gas with no intermediate liquid state.   It is said to "sublime" on heating, that is; the application of heat vapourises the solid.

The term "contradiction" is also used loosely, to describe irreconciliable opposites of a social or economic character. This usage is to be distinguished from the "formal contradiction" of logic discovered by Aristotle, the way most people normally use the term.

For instance, increase in population coincident with decrease in food supply is a "contradiction" which must be resolved by either decrease in population or increase in food production or both together.

An obvious contradiction is that of Male and Female, Yin and Yang, the unity of both resulting in offspring either male or female; but not both, with the exception of hermaphroditic species which are simultaneously male and female or alternately male or female.

The most general antitheses in Nature are such as are described by Life and Non-Life, Matter and consciousness; Material and Ideal, Truth and Falsehood.

The essence of dialectic contradiction is contained in the question:-

"Which came first the egg or the chicken"?

and is exemplified in the continuity-discontinuity dichotomy of the nature of space and time underlying Zeno's paradoxes.

Examples of the contradictory nature of reality are also exemplified by the pairs:-

Appearance and Essence.

Form and Content.

Necessity and Chance.

Certainty and Impossibility.

Finite and Infinite.

Absolute and Relative.

Unity and Plurality.

Continuity and Discontinuity.

Conflict and Harmony.

II.   TRANSFORMATION OF QUANTITY INTO QUALITY.

This principle asserts that a continuing increase or decrease
in the measurements of quantity of any anything; that is an
increased aggregation of an entity or quality of an entity on
a continuous basis can and often does result in qualitative
change or transformation of the substance or quality at some
given accretion of quantity.

The very structure of matter itself is replete with examples of
the law. We have already seen that the addition of quantities
of heat will turn a solid into liquid or a liquid into gas.
We can go deeper!

If we consider atomic number in relation to how atoms of the
various chemical elements are composed we discover a startling
example of this law in operation.

The atomic number of an element is the number of protons or
electrons comprising the atoms structure.   It would seem
reasonable that if the atomic number of an element increases we
would have a new, heavier but similar element.   This is true
only within limits. If we increase the atomic number of sodium
from 11 to 16 we have sulphur. If however, we increase the
atomic number of sulphur to 17 we obtain chlorine gas. If we
increase the atomic number of Iodine from 53 to 54 we get the
inert gas Xenon.

If we increase the atomic number of Oxygen from 8 to 12 we get metallic mercury. In a mere primitive example we can assert that if four men can build a house in one month, sixteen men will not build four houses, but perhaps five or six houses in a month. This law is related to the concept of Holism which asserts that the whole is much more than the mere amalgamation or sum of its constitutent parts.

III. NEGATION OF THE NEGATION.

This law asserts that if a particular condition, relationship or structure is negated or turned into its opposite either partly or wholly, due to material or social conditions, it may be at a later historical stage again negated in whole or in part and return to its origional condition, albeit at a higher level.

Two classic examples are:

(1)   The communal ownership of property being negated to bring private ownership of wealth and class society into existence and the subsequent negation of capitalism and the return to social ownership or Socialism.

(2)   The development from polygamy to monogamy and monogamy back to polygamy via serial monogamy.

The above described three laws are original to Frederick Engels.

The exposition here given is unique to the author.

V.   RATIONAL LAWS.

1.   MENTAL IMAGES and IDEAS activate the person.

2.   MENTAL IMAGES and IDEAS generate EMOTIONS and corresponding ATTITUDES.

3.   Actions tend to generate related EMOTIONS, ATTITUDES and IMAGES.

4.   EMOTIONS and ATTITUDES tend to awaken and intensify corresponding MENTAL IMAGES and EMOTIONS.

5.   Resolutions of THOUGHT process result in resolutions of EMOTION STRUCTURE.

6.   NEEDS, DRIVES AND DESIRES tend to arouse corresponding IMAGES, IDEAS AND EMOTIONS.

7.   Attention, spontaneous or developed interest, affirmation and repetition all reinforce IMAGES, ATTITUDES and EMOTION on which they are centred.

8.   Repetition results in habituation and renders the execution of tasks easy and automatic.

9.   All our innate NEEDS, DESIRES and DRIVES adopt subconscious strategies for their satisfaction in line with or against conscious volition.

10.   NEEDS, DESIRES AND DRIVES but especially, EMOTIONS demand expression or assertion.

11.   The Association Of Ideas,Facts And Emotions.

The first associations of colour, form, sound, taste and touch come to us from Nature through the senses.

Associations become internally organised in human consciousness in a way that reflects their organisation in Nature.

Sensory images are associated on the basis of their contiguity in experience; their similarity and contrast.

All sensory images have affective components and all derivative mental images retain this emotive element in consciousness.

Mental images and ideas find association on the basis of similiarity , commonality and contrast and the relationship of their affective content in consciousness, as a primary aspect.

We can have association on the basis of judgements of opposites as well as similarity;

E.G.

> Love and Hate
> Beauty and Ugliness
> Hot and Cold
> Dark and Bright

all find association as pairs on the basis of their connection as opposites.

Beauty and ugliness find association through their affective components, with love and hate.

We tend to have a generalised association of all things we love and of all things we hate.

This generalised association operates on all the emotions.

The generalised association of things on the basis of common emotions is Affective Association.

We also tend to have a generalised association of all things that we perceive as similar , disimilar or opposite.

This is Rational Association.

We tend to have a generalised association of things which occur together in space and time.

This is Empirical Association.

Regarding affective association,it can be said that positive and negative feelings, constructive and destructive attitudes,sthenic and asthenic emotions; can all be associated with mental images and ideas of moral right and wrong.

The association of emotion with ideas of right and wrong is called cathechism.

We can be right in two important ways:-

We can be right in our thinking and

We can be right in how we feel about our thought.

The Affective , Empirical and Rational associations of consciousness over periods of personal development all become integrated and related more or less strongly.

These associations, underwritten by the memory form the basis of philosophical capacity.

The other ingredient is logic as intrinsic to human mental processes.

The rational mind is a harmony of thought process and emotional experience,resulting in behavioural stability and the absence of eccentricity or fanaticism.

Rational association is inseparable from the processes of mental judgement and the logical interconnection of ideas.

All events requiring similar types of judgement or logical processes become associated in memory inevitably.

All things of unique or discrete emotional impact find association on the basis of similarity, commonality and disimilarity and are linked with their concrete objects in the external world as experienced over time and retained in the memory.

All things causally related in Nature and Society ultimately find association in the human consciousness and memory; reflecting observed regularities in Nature and Society.

MODES OR EXPRESSION OF THE WILL.

1.   It's intensity or the degree of effort expendable in overcoming obstacles to one's aims.

2.   It's endurance and persistence.

3.   The degree and end of it's regulation of personal consciousness and character.

POLES OF PERSONALITY:

Appolonian   versus   Dionysian.

Epicurean   versus   Stoic.

Self disclosing versus Concealing.

Expressive   versus   Unexpressive.

In the mid point or harmony between these roles of personality SELF MASTERY is to be attained.

4.   The quality of concentration and attention, mental and sensory; voluntary and involuntary.

5. Decisiveness.

6. Resoluteness.

7. Determination.

8   Patience.

9. Persistence.

10. Organisation, integration and synthesis of the foregoing (1 - 9).

Willpower requires:

(a) Self Respect.

(b) A Self Ideal.

(c) A General Goal in Life.

(d) Organised and habitual creative and positive activity or work.

Willpower is the actualisation of our Desires and Intentions for ourselves and others.

(e) **Outer Expression.**

Examples of this are:

(I) Compassion effected through humanitarian action.

(II) Aggression or Hatred turned against evil or injustice.

(III) Love effected in constructive social or practical work.

(f) **Suggestion.**

Auto-suggestion works on the subconscious mind, independent of consciousness and can be an effective tool of self improvement, change and regeneration.

(g) **Action.**

All human activity falls under the category of action. The manifestation and expression of the self in action of any kind such as is moral is a major source of happiness and satisfaction as well as a means to the perfection of talents and abilities.

11.   Psychological Energies find expression through:-

(a) Direct Discharge or CATHARSIS.

(b) Indirect Discharge or SYMBOLIC ACTION. Symbolic
     Action requires a symbol at which catharsis
     would otherwise be directed.

(c) Transmutation. Transmutation of psychological
     energy finds it expression in physical or
     bio-social action.

(d) "Sublimation" and "Sensualisation".

     "Sublimation" is the projection of psychological
     energies into practically useful work of a moral,
     aesthetic or creative artistic or scientific type.

     "Sensualisation" is the reverse of "Sublimation";
     it is the projection of psychological energies
     into physical and biological satisfactions.

EXAMPLES:-

          DESIRE AND AFFECTION - LUST AND TENDERNESS;
          May be "sublimated" into Romantic Love.
          Romantic Love may find it's "sensualisation" in
          sexual intercourse with one's love partner.
          Natural Biological Needs may be "sublimated"
          morally into charitable work.

          Authentic Social Work may be "sensualised"
          spontaneously into the satisfaction of
          bio-social needs and drives.
          The affective or emotional, lies intermediate to
          "Sublimation" and "Sensualisation" of
          psychological energies and is a more normal
          condition of human consciousness.

12.   **Psychological Transformation is achieved through:-**

(a) **ELEVATION.**

For example:-

      (I)   biological needs and the sexual drive can be elevated into emotional love.

      (II)   Love-longing can be elevated into the creation of romantic music, art or literature.

      (III) Sensuous pleasure can be elevated into the aesthetic appreciation of Nature, Art or Music.

(b) Purification is essentially the moral assessment of motives and goals. It can also be the reduction of aims to be in harmony with one's true nature and self.

(c) Interiorisation is the containment of aggression, assertion, lust and appetite or emotion in general such as transmutes it.

      E.G: Vanity can be transmuted into dignity. Self Aggresion can be turned against one's vices to eliminate them.

(d) Extension is the expansion of Self Love to encompass Humanity as it's object. We cannot love ourselves without loving common Humanity and vice versa.

ASPECTS OF THE WILL.

1. It's relative strength or weakness.

2. It's degree of INTELLIGENCE in utilising aspects of conscious so as to support and reinforce itself.

3. The content of the WILL.

4. There is the WILL to:-

    (a) Good or Evil or neither Good nor Evil.

    (b) The WILL to survival.

    (c) The WILL to sex and reproduction.

    (d) The WILL to LOVE and be LOVED.

    (e) The WILL to HATRED and destruction.

    (f) The WILL to emotional experience and expression.

    (g) The WILL to satisfaction of natural NEEDS and DESIRES.

    (h) The WILL to POWER and FREEDOM.

    (i) The WILL to KNOWLEDGE and WORK.

    (j) The WILL to LIFE and ACTION.

    (k) The WILL to VIRTUE and MORAL living.

    (l) The WILL to Self Realisation and Happiness.

VI.   WILL.

1.   To change the course of action requires re-organisation
      of   our   activities   in   the   light   of   NEW   IDEALS.

2.   Ideals   must   be   realistic   and   authentic to ourselves.

3.   To retrieve WILL POWER one   must   retrieve   one's   self
      respect.

4.   Action   fixes   habit. Control, use or dominate your
      moods.

5.   WILL the POSSIBLE and it may come true.

6.   Organise the CONVERGENCE of your aims.

7.   Seek the achievement of all ORDINARILY necessary things.

8.   Identify   your   aims,   needs   and   desires   and thereby
      strengthen your WILL.

9.   Because we are not good at everything does not   mean   we
      are good at nothing.

10.   Seek the satisfaction of all natural needs and   desires;
      they are essentially moral.

11.   Inconsistency   where   it is a break from false or
      delusional   orthodoxy is good where it results in
      enlightenment or self improvement.

12.   Lack of POWER may be due to repressed   FEAR,   GUILT   or
      DESIRES.

13.   Try to KNOW and BE yourself.

14.   Be and Do; nor merely admire and appreciate.

15.   Face the cost and sacrifice involved in achievement.

16.   Bad habits are broken by running away from them.

17.   Study carefully, both your failures and successes.

18.   Good habits are the basis of moral character.

19.   Imagination is the single most powerful instrument of
achievement and progress.

VII.   THE STRUCTURE OF THE WILL.

1.   Integrate all the aspects of CONSCIOUSNESS,unifying it.

2.   Identify the EGO or SELF, the "I" at the centre and
focus of these aspects.

3.   WILL exists as a distinct and autonomous activity of the
EGO or "I".

4.   Through the WILL the "I" or EGO directs and regulates
(both consciously and unconsciously) all aspects of
consciousness; sensory, emotional and mental; insofar as
is possible.

SELF REALISATION

I : INTRODUCTION

CONSCIOUSNESS

Personal being is essentially the individuals consciousness and
their consciousness is combined in three aspects. Firstly,
there is sensation or everything which stimulates the senses;
secondly, there is mentality or thought and thirdly there is
emotion. Emotion is that aspect of consciousness inseparable
from physical senation which is the arena of interaction of
sensation and mentality. Both sense perception and mental
perception, or the faculties that select, differientiate and
integrate what is held in the sense and the mind have affective
consequences. Colours and shapes and sounds and substances or
objects touched all produce emotive responses as do mental
images. In general, the psyche or consciousness in its
operation is an integrated whole where there is correspondence
between the various senses regarding what is perceived, between
the sense consciousness generally impressed and mental images
of it also. It is for our consideration most important to
realise that sense consciousness and mental consciousness in
what is perceived sensually or mentally is of emotional
consequence at all times.

The emotions are possibly one of the most determining aspects
of the individuals actions. Emotions may be sthenic or
aesthenic; that is, they may be joyful or sorrowful. They may
be activating or immobilising. We all know that in many
circumstances emotion controls our behaviour such that
irrespective of what we are thinking or would like to do, we
are compelled to act in directions ordered by our emotional
responses to situations and people. The basic emotions which
we all feel from time to time are Love and Hate, Vanity and
Humility, Fear and Anger, Envy and Jealousy and they all have
an important role to play in determining our activity. The

emotions have a rationale of their own and are involuntary
responses usurping our will in their operation. Emotions may
be constructive and healthy or destructive and unhealthy in
certain extreme cases. Love and Hate, Fear and Anger are
opposites and all strong emotion tends to become a generalised
response. If we love we tend to love everyone and everything
likewise if we hate we tend to hate everyone and everything.
In the extremes, we reach blind love or hatred both of which
are unhealthy and contradictory. If we love the opposite of
what we hate and love and hate discriminately and in a balanced
fashion then we will remain rational. For example to love
beauty or truth is to hate ugliness or falsehood and vice-
versa. It is so with all the emotions, they must be
subservient to rational control of some degree and they are in
the thinking person, if they are not to dominate us in
unhealthy discord. When we learn to be emotionally
discriminate and "think with the heart" or have our thinking
processes integrated harmoniously in their varied aspects with
our emotions then we are rational beings. Thought may result
in emotion as emotion may provoke thought and emotion as we
have suggested may be instigated by sensory perceptions also.
Rage and terror are examples of extreme anger and fear where
the mental aspect of consciousness has surrendered to the
sensuous and emotional, such extreme states are generally
dangerous and unhealthy for the person experiencing them.

THE SUBCONSCIOUS

The existence of memory is evidence of the existence of the
subconscious and the unconscious intervention of what we have
learned or been conditioned to, in many aspects of our
behaviour, determines how we react, to as great an extent and
in some instances to a greater extent than conscious; sensory,
emotional or mental responses to situations. The subconscious
is built up of memories that were once part of our
consciousness, which we remember or have forgotten, yet operate

on our behaviour; or aspects which were never really conscious but through suggestion became part of our subconscious; affect our behaviour and may never readily be retrieved from our subconscious.

Our behaviour is determined by the interaction of our subconscious and conscious mentality, sensations and perceptions along with aspects of these which comprise learned or conditioned behaviour patterns.

CONDITIONING

Conditioning is the effect of the external environment in altering our consciousness and subconscious and thereby altering our subsequent behaviour to recurrent objective circumstances. Conditioning does not affect the mentality of the individual in so far as it determines behaviour as an aspect of consciousness; it operates in the area of sensation and emotion. Conditioning elicits involuntary emotional responses such as fear or anger or particular drives such as hunger or thirst which largely determine the nature of situational behaviour. One will have a conscious or unconscious memory of previous situations; these memories have affective and mental as well as sensational aspects. However, the affective and sensational only, play a significant part in conditioning.

We can exert our mentality and go against our conditioned responses to a situation and become active or passive as a consequence, in a way in which if we merely responded as conditioned we might behave very differently. Conditioning is to a large extent emotional learning and is based on such things as fear, aggression, sexual response, hunger, vanity etc.,

SELF-KNOWLEDGE

The knowledge of oneself only comes through introspection and reflection regarding how we are in our active lives in all the various situations in which we recurrently find ourselves. We may not know whether we are a dominantly emotional or thinking person; though most will; but we know how we respond in certain situations to stimuli and suggestions if we care to reflect on memories and analyse them. With regard to changing our behaviour or activity or altering our responses to certain situations there is no substitute for self knowledge; indeed the degree of self-knowledge and awareness of the individual is a major factor in assessing their maturity and degree of fulfillment as a person.

THE PERSON

Every person is a combination of four aspects. Appearance, Mentality, Personality and Sexuality. People are attracted or repelled to one another of the same sex or of the opposite sex on the basis of these four aspects. Every person has an Ego, that which is unconscious of itself while thinking and of a 'self' or the mental image of the whole person which is oneself. This image may be objective and accurate or fanciful or deluded and the extent to which a persons 'self' or self image is objective is a measure of their social experience and maturity. The 'self image' and its degree of constancy or development is a major factor of our personality development.

SELF REALISATION

Self realisation is the attainment of mature self awareness and self knowledge by the individual and the application of this knowledge to the full development and fulfillment of the person in life. It is the realisation in achievement of the positive and valuable qualities of the person and the attainment of happiness and the good or the escape from suffering in life not caused by material deprivation, physical illness, or the loss of loved ones.

II : GENERAL ASPECTS

HEALTH

Health is physical, emotional and mental in its aspects and the moderate continuous exercise of these aspects of the person are essential to its maintenance. Nutrition, exercise of mind and body and the education of the senses and emotions are all essential to ongoing health. Balance of the physical, emotional and mental aspects of the person and their harmonious integration in useful and pleasurable or rewarding activity are equally imperative. Recurrent sexual functioning and orgasm; such that pregenital or aesthetic aspects and genital or conjugal aspects of sexuality are fulfilled along with parenthood, are highly desireable for mental, emotional and physcial health. Wellbeing and spirituality cannot be based on the abuse or neglect or ill health of either mind, body or emotions.

OBJECTIVE MENTAL ATTITUDE

An objective mental attitude is such 'mental set' as contains conative and affective aspects as are indispensible for the solution of the general problems of living, occupation and activity. It is impossible to achieve anything without the will to ahcieve and the correct mental attitude. Both excessive optimism and pessimism are eschewed by the correct mental set.

NATURAL SELF REGULATION

Natural self regulation is the individual, convenient, reiterate pattern of daily activity. That is work, rest, eating, drinking, defecation, urination and sexual copulation. The underlying determinant of natural self regulation is sex economy or the frequency and kind of sexual activity.

SELF DISCIPLINE

Only such discipline as is necessary and aids rather than hinders natural self regulation of the individual is desirable.

EXTERNAL DISCIPLINE

External discipline is such discipline as is essential to the completion and fulfillment of the individuals objective survival whether this discipline is naturally imposed or is artifically regulated and collective activity.

GENERAL DISCIPLINE

Discipline should be an integration of External and Self discipline, each augmenting the other and must be limited to that which is necessary for health and happiness and moderate and balanced pursuit of goals.

THE WILL

Will is the capacity to generate and direct ones energies. It is a capacity to render ones immediate inclinations subservient to one's immediate or long term goals. The over-exercise of the will undermines the operation of the innate intelligence of a person or mental ability. Self suggestion and curiosity are great instruments for strengthening the operation of the will. Goals must embody one's genuine inclinations and dispositions of interest if they are to be attained.

DESIRES

Happiness is the fulfillment of moral desire as unhapiness is the frustration or perversion of moral desire. All desire has a natural end and consequence and serves the survival and health of the species, relating activity to species needs. Only death brings about the end of desire; the desire for the end of desire is a death wish.

PAIN AND PLEASURE

Anything which is solely the cause of pleasure and causes no pain is good. Anything which is solely the cause of pain and causes no pleasure is bad. The absence of pain and pleasure both is neither good nor bad.

That which solely causes both pain pleasure is good and bad.

Pleasure causing pain is bad?

Pain resulting in pleasure is good?

GOALS:

Every individual will have conscious and particular goals in life different from those of other people. However, everyone must have goals in general and which we all hold in common, if we are to lead the good and fulfilling life.

Our first aim in life and our total aim in life is the satisfaction of natural needs. The needs we seek to satisfy are determined and evidenced by such rational conscious or unconscious motivations as people have and they are:-

(1) Physiological Needs.

(2) The need to express lust and aggression and the need for sex.

(3) The pursuit of pleasure and the avoidance of pain.

(4) Expression and experience of emotion. Love and Hate, Fear and Anger, Vanity and Humility, Envy and Jealousy.

(5) The desire for self preservation.

(6) The attainment of freedom and power.

(7) Material and emotional security.

(8) Material Gain.

(9) Achievement and self actualisation or fulfillment.

(10) Honour or status and recognition.

WISDOM:

The most important wisdom is that virtue is the key to happiness. The pursuit of wisdom will ultimately reveal this truth to anyone. Virtue is the pursuit of Truth and the application of truth to the wellbeing of ourselves; others and Humanity generally. Virtue is neither good nor is it evil. What is good is that which results from the practice of virtue. The human virtues are:-

(1)	Prudence.	(2)	Fortitude.
(3)	Temperance and moderation.	(4)	Justice in dealing with everyone.
(5)	Kindness.	(6)	Courage.
(7)	Liberality.	(8)	Honesty and Integrity.
		(9)	Loyalty.

Buddhists describe virtue in terms of 'right being' which they perceptively describe as follows:-

(1) Right Thinking; comprising right vision, right mindfulness and right concentration.

(a) Right vision is the perception of the causes of pain and suffering.

(b) Right Mindfulness, is the concentration and attentive examination of consciousness such that one can learn to control the affective aspects of consciousness and so eliminate subjective causes of suffering and pain.

(c)   Right concentration is the process of solipsist
        meditation whereby the person attains a state that is
        neither of wellbeing nor suffering and devoid of thought.

(2)   Right Purpose, that is to aim at and intend harmlessness
        or non violence and to aspire to the attainment of Truth,
        Justice, Beauty, Freedom and Love, that is, the
        attainment of virtue.

(3)   Right Speech, or to speak only truth, to speak without
        anger or harshness or vulgarity.

(4)   Right Action is to refarin from taking life, to be proper
        in sexual relationships and social affairs and not to
        steal.

(5)   Right Livelihood or to earn ones living, honestly and in
        an occupation suited to ones nature and abilities and
        exert oneself suitably.

(6)   Right Association, or to associate only with honest and
        virtuous people.

(7)   Right Effort or one strives for the attainment of
        wholesome and rational states of consciousness and
        activity.

(8)   Right memory or one strives for retention, recall and
        recognition of significant aspects of thought and
        experience.

These eight canons loosely interpreted here are known as the
Eightfold Path to the cessation of suffering and ultimately
Nirvana.

        Knowledge and Action both are essential to success.
          The causes of failure are ignorance, stupidity,
                      vanity and laziness.

HAPPINESS AND SUFFERING:

Happiness is something we all seek to attin of and suffering we all wish to escape. It is obvious that no one can be happy all the time and that some suffering is inevitable for all of us. The realisation that suffering is passing as well as happiness and that we can reasonably aspire to a greater measure of happiness than suffering in life is a source of contentment. Happiness may be negatively described as the absence of suffering and vice-versa. Positively thinking we can say that the fulfillment of the person and the good life is happiness.

THE CAUSES OF SUFFERING:

As we well know, in order to achieve happiness we must know what it is and how to pursue it.

Secondly, we must know the causes of suffering and how to avoid them. Pain is suffering and pleasure wellbeing.

The Causes of Suffering are as follows:-

(1) Unfilled Love longing.

(2) Fear based on Ignorance.

(3) Craving for the unattainable.

(4) Craving for illusory good, based on ignorance of the true good.

(5) Ignorance of necessity.

(6) Preoccupation with the 'self' distinct from Egocentrism.

(7) Selfishness and Greed.

(8) Vanity.

(9) Injustice.

(10) Being unloved.

(11) Being incapable of love.

(12) Immorality of any kind.

In considering happiness it is inescapably true that one who is unloved or incapable of love is lonely and unhappy and that with love the viscissitudes of life are greatly reduced in significance and easily endurable.

Remember:

(1)   If the man is right his life will be right and vice versa.

(2)   Trust yourself not to be immoral and you won't be.

(3)   If you trust your very basic perceptions, feelings and thinking you will automatically live right.

III   :   A PHILOSOPHY FOR LIVING:

When one thinks for oneself and answers such questions generally posed by living, for oneself; one is being a philosopher. This is a very difficult thing to do. We must analyse our own experiences, ask and answer questions regarding them and taking heed of a lot of readily given and available opinion or advice, form our own judgments. Philosophy means literally 'love of wisdom' and a love of wisdom is a precondition for its pursuit and attainment. In the pursuit of wisdom or knowledge which would enable us to be better judges of what is our own best interest or humanity's best interest for that matter, we are all faced with our own limitations of intellect, education and circumstances. The perception of what those limitations are is a first priority if we are to reduce or overcome those limitations. Thinking is the most worthwhile activity any of us can engage in and a mind turned inward on itself or outward at natural and social realities can gain great insights and attain much knowledge. However, the thinking of other people is great food for the development of our own intellect and conversation with anyone on topics in

which we wish to become learned and the selective reading of
books on related subject matter will greatly accelerate our
learning and develop it to a greater extent tha if we neglect
these areas.   An acquaintance with philosophy as a formal
subject, though requiring much reading and effort; along with
the basics of psychology is exceptionally rewarding.   Of
paramount importance for the individual who would think for
themselves is the subject of logic, which is an investigation
of the forms of valid thinking or thinking devoid of wrong or
fallacious arument. Notwithstanding, it would be a mistake to
stereotype our thinking in the best structures of formal logic
entirely, as the human mind is capable of a wide range of
logical operations which are as yet undiscovered; nor will the
logical capacities and range of the human mind ever be
exhausted by humans. Academic or pure philosophy is one thing;
the application of knowledge to the solution of the problems of
living or applied philosophy is another matter.   We can all
assimilate knowledge, but the acquisition of knowledge will not
make us act wisely of itself alone. We must think in every
situation or about every problem we face in a practical and
fortright manner.   We must mentally attack our problems and
persist in this practice until we see solutions and then put
the solutions into practice and act.

Thought of itself, while it is a most rewarding exercise from
the point of view of the pleasure derived and the insight
gained, if not backed up by subsequent action is a fairly
sterile pursuit which changes us as persons while it little
affects our circumstances, except where changes in the person
spur them to action.   Thus it is necessary to engage in
thought, study and communication, but action of a practical and
purposeful nature is of paramount importance. Additionally, we
must endeavour that there is balance between the various
aspects of our activity and the determination of the balance of
these activities and the extent to which we engage in any
particular one's must be the degree of success or failure we
experience in the pursuit of our aims.

Of importance in deciding what we should engage in and to what
extent is for many of us a matter of curiosity, interest or
mood. We should follow our curiosity and interests while they
are alive and use our moods to propel us into such activities
which we find pleasurable as a consequence of our moods,
wherever possible. It is important to realise that an
integration of physical and mental activity such as maintains
enthusiasm; through keeping our emotions alive and healthy is
essential to all undertakings. Music, song and dance, the
Arts, Sciences and Humanities together are important in the
development, nuture and maintenance of a healthy outlook on
life. The excessive pursuit of any one of these to the neglect
of others, leads to staleness and loss of enthusiasm for
living. We must endeavour to be complete individuals, neither
narrow nor lop-sided in our development. We do not have to
attain to professional status in all spheres of activity as
this would be impossibly difficult and time consuming for most
people. We should however, cultivate a wide range of leisure
interests which we indulge in for the sake of the pleasured
variety of the activities. We will find as a consequence an
enrichment of the whole personality. We all find particular
abilities the exercise of which brings us inordinate pleasure
and success and it is in these areas that we should find our
livelihood and main occupation. The pursuit of wisdom and the
experience of love, joy, tranquility, equanimity and vigour are
all essential to our enlightenment and happiness. We should
mix actively and widely yet always reserve a period of solitude
for reflection and meditation each day. We must follow our
hearts and allow the head to serve the heart and guide our
activity.

Engage in thought, study, communication and wide general
activity. Pursue the Sciences, Arts and Humanities in relation
to our likes and interests. Keep philosophy in the driving
seat and apply its insights to the positive change and
improvement of ourselves and our situation in life.

IV THERAPEUTIC AUTOPSYCHOLOGY

Autopsychology is the self application of psychology to eliminate one's emotional problems and personality inadequacies. The catergories under which one can proceed are psychoanalysis and hypnotism, counter-conditioning and meditation.

(a) PSYCHOANALYSIS AND SELF HYPNOTISM:

There are three aspects to the personality of the individual; Ego, Id, Super-Ego and two aspects to the individual mind as it affects behaviour; conscious mind or thought and subconscious mind. Then there is Libido or that which powers all aspects of the personality.

Ego is that which thinks and is unconscious of itself while doing so.

Id is the basic instinctual aspect of the person which seeks to be aggressive or gratify itself sexually, to seek pleasure and to avoid pain.

Super-Ego is the conscience of the individual.

In the normal and happy individual the Id and Super-Ego are in harmony with one another through the operation of the Ego. This harmonious integration may be called Ego-centrism and in which the individual pursues their goals without guilt and without emotional disturbance or upset. Ego-centrism is dominantly a rationalistic outlook where the individual is geared to responses to the real situations in which they find themselves, in line with their own interests and in which there is harmony of thought and emotion in expressed or dominating attitudes. Libido, is that which powers the operation and integration of Super-Ego, Ego and Id and is the life force of the individual, it has a powerful sexual aspect, particularly in relation to reproductive needs.

Conscious and subconscious mind are the two aspects of mentality and both interact in so far as they determine our behaviour. Where the subconscious mind holds unresolved conflicts regarding issues of conscience, the self image, or any aspect of intention or learning, a state of disharmony exists between conscious and subconscious mentality and personality disorder, neurosis or psychosis is prevalent in our behaviour patterns. The conscious mind is affected and influenced by conscious perceptions as is the subconsicous in its memory of these. However, the subconscious can be influenced by suggestion which can by-pass the conscious mind. The harmonious integration of conscious and subconscious mind and the resolution and therefore absence of subconscious conflicts is essential to well being.

(1)   Inhibitions generated by the subconscious mind influence behaviour.

(2)   Such inhibitions may be emotionally protective except where they are the product of phantasms.

(3)   Phantasms are false impressions accepted by the conscious or unconscious mind as true.

(4)   Phantasms disappear either if one ignores them or presents facts and agruments contrary to what they assert.

(5)   Subconscious inhibitions can be displaced by positive influence of the subconscious mind, through suggestion; in line with conscious desires and we can thus erase or eliminate subconscious inhibitions and conflicts and substitute positive volitional action powered by the subconscious for immobilising hesitation.

(6)   Subconscious Teleology is the method used to about bring about these changes.Teleology is the doctrine that events are due ultimately to the purpose they serve.

(7)   Subconscious Teleology works independently of the conscious mind.

(8)   The sensitivity of the subconscious mind to external influence is greatest when the conscious mind is less active.

(9)   Auto-suggestion (or self-hypnotism) employed while the subconscious mind is receptive is highly potent. It should be in the direct positive form.

(10)   Mind affects the operation of the body and vice-versa through the emotions. Physical and mental consciousness are intercausally related.

(11)   The conscious mind controls the subconscious; though the subconscious also directs the operation of the conscious mind.

(12)   The conscious mind and subconscious mind together operating in co-operation rather than conflict, produce a 'state of being' conducive to satisfaction and happiness.

(13)   A state of subconscious conflict hinders or prevents a satisfactory 'state of being' existing.

(14)   The subconscious mind demands superiority and control over external realities.

(15)   Subconscious Conflicts are changed by:

       (a) Action   (b) Mentabolism or change of mind.

(16)   Mentabolism consists in changing any particular feeling, by altering the mental image inspiring it.

(17) Habits are the results of mental images and can be changed by altering the images underlying them or substituting other related images.

(18) The attention can be voluntarily and involuntarily controlled.

(19) By control of attention, the selective determinant of consciousness (mental and physical) we can control the affective consequences of our perceived environment.

(20) Both sensory and mental perceptions have affective consequences.

(21) Perception is the interface of the subjective and objective realities.

(22) Both sensory and mental perceptions 'infer' the nature of reality and to that extent are subjective.

(23) We can choose to see what is relevant to our security, needs or happiness in any situation or vice-versa.

(24) By control of imagination, contrasting negative and positive, pessimistic and optimistic we can control our emotional state ensuring neither elation nor depression.

(25) By control of our thinking or mental state (conscious and subconscious) we can control our emotions and feelings.

(26) If we thus ensure our emotional stability, we do not experience extremes of feeling and we can refuse to allow either people or circumstances to induce excess of self destructive feeling; our mental state as a consequence being rational and objective.

(27) Sensory and mental perceptions both are always to some
extent subjective. We must learn to perceive things as
objectively as possible both in their positive and
negative aspects.

(28) Feelings can be controlled by thought and thought usurped
by feeling. It is a quention of conscious and
subconscious mentality and physical sensation.

(29) We must guard against suggestion or auto-suggestion and
imagination of an excessively optimistic or pessimistic
nature. 'Beware the lie by suggestion'.

(30) It is undesirable to 'bottle up' our feelings, all
feelings should find expression in assertive manner
whether direct or indirect and must not be repressed.

(31) We must learn to lend mobility and flexibility to our
emotions and feelings.

(32) We must aim at the expression of our perceptions, thought
and feelings in integrated and unified activity.

(33) Extremes of feeling are generally harmless except where
they usurp our rational functioning.

(34) Psychic energy is a mighty force and its magnitude is
proportional to its degree of employment.

(35) Intense feelings (eg., hatred or fear) have a tendency
to become generalised. It is essential to be
discriminate in our feeling as much as in our thinking.

(36) Volitional cathexis (or the deliberate forcing of ideas
as correct or incorrect) results in fanaticism.

(37) Excessive volitional attention or 'obsessional observation' of sensory and perceptual stimuli results in psychic disintegration.

(38) Obvious aspects of personality type to the perceptive observer are:

(a) The general degree of situational Extroversion versus Introversion.

(b) In relation to the three aspects of consciousness whether the individual is dominantly an emotional, sensational or thinking person or whether as an aspect of mentality they are dominantly intuitive or logical.

(39) DEFENCE MECHANISMS.

Emotionally immature individuals tend to use the 'defence mechanisms' as a means of coping with social realities and personal inadequacies which they would otherwise fail to cope with. The perceptive obersver will again notice their operation possibly in themselves and in others. To a significant extent, they are as follows:-

(1) The repression of emotions, impulses and 'dangerous' ideas.

(2) Irrational inhibitions, particularly regarding sexual matters and emotive responses to plain talking and honesty regarding sexuality.

(3) Reaction Formation or the substitution of opposite feelings for one's truely felt eg. saying 'I hate you' when they really mean 'I love you' but can't cope with that reality.

(4) Projection or for example saying 'You hate me'
     when they really mean 'I hate you' but can't cope
     with this.

(5) Fixation or the fact that behaviour, particularly
     sexual behaviour is frozen at the level suitable
     to an earlier stage of the individuals development
     eg., a thirty year old with teenage attitudes and
     behaviour patterns.

(6) Regression or the return by a mature individual to
     the attitudes and personality patterns of their
     youthful selves.

(7) Displacement for example allowing ones interests
     in subject or person A to be displaced to subject
     or person B because A is difficult or
     unobtainable though we have little interest in B.

(8) Rationalisation. Making excuses for and explaining
     away our inadequacies.

(9) Compensation or satisfying a need because a
     different need is frustrated, eg., choosing to be
     dignified because we can't be the outgoing
     personality we would like to be.

(b) BEHAVIOUR MODIFICATION:

Under psychoanalysis and self hypnotism, I described methods for tackling emotional and personality problems. In this section I repeat this intention but tackle the problem from the point of view of behaviourist psychology.

If a person can be conditioned to particular responses or behaviour patterns whether normal or neurotic, they can be conditioned out of such responses or 'de-conditioned'. If for instance a person has been conditioned to pleasurable sexual responses by a discotheque environment and music, they can be conditioned to aversion to the same and vice-versa.

There are various types of psychological conditioning and they fall into the following categories:-

(1) Classical or Pavlovian conditioning.

(2) Operational Conditioning.

(3) Purposive Conditioning.

(4) Instrumental Conditioning.

The interested reader would be well advised to follow up these categories in a text book of psychology. Our treatment of the subject matter will be elementary and aimed at the illustration of the fact that conditioned behaviour can be de-conditioned. We shall deal with three categories of conditioning.

(1) If a stimulus which generates a pleasurable emotional response or a drive response in the individual is frequently paired with an arbitrary stimulus; the latter stimulus will, if operating alone, be enough to trigger the original response of itself, subsequently. Thus if we frequent a discotheque and experience a particular type of music along with gratification of sexual needs, in time the type of music alone will turn us on sexually and we may expect sexual gratification. If however the same music become associated with sexual frustration subsequently the original conditioning affect of the music becomes nullified and of course the opposite case would equally rule where music associated with sexually frustrating experiences became subsequently associated with sexually gratifying experiences. We have mentioned (a) gratification and (b) frustration. If the causes of gratification of our needs become associated with some arbitrary environmental factor, the presence of this factor alone will cause us to anticipate the gratification of those needs. Likewise the frustration of our needs becoming associated with some environmental factor (either physical or social) will tend to cause us to expect the frustration of our needs.

If we become aware of this conditioning it is important to realise that is can be overcome by the substitution of frustration for gratification or vice-versa in relation to the common conditioning stimulus. The conditioning effect originally produced is thus rapidly extinguished. It will become extinguished over time lapses between the experience of the same type of situation anyway, but it may also recover spontaneously.

If we find ourselves in a situation where spontaneously expressed behaviour is rewarded or punished that behaviour will be reinforced or strengthened or it will be extinguished. The substitution of reward for punishment or vice-versa will result in de-conditioning us to such operant conditioning.

SYSTEMATIC DESENSITISATION

If a particular stimulus always elicits a particular type of response from us, eg., shyness on meeting a person in authority, with wealth or who is a beautiful specimen of the opposite sex; by gradually introducing us to the stimulus (in this case a person) more frequently in pleasant and sociable or reassuring circumstances, we will gradually lose our shyness with regard to this particular person.   Secondly, if we but imagine ourselves introduced to such people and responding confidently repeatedly, we will lose our shyness also.

FLOODING

Flooding is the process where a person is introduced suddenly into a situation they fear and the consequent emotional response in mastering the situation effaces any possibility of subsequent fear of the situation.   A typical example is throwing a person who is 'afraid of the water' into the deep end of the swimming pool. They may learn to swim and float suddenly and never fear the water again. However, they might just drown and there is always some inherent danger of failure in emotional flooding; but in many instances it works successfully. One can imagine a person overcoming stage fright this way, but can equally imagine them retaining a worse case of stage fright subsequently. It is a risky business after all and not to be too often resorted to.

NEGATIVE PRACTICE

Negative practice is the operation of repeating unwanted behaviour to the point where it becomes extinguished.

ASSERTIVE TRAINING

Assertive training is the operation of encouraging people with emotional problems consequent of repressive experiences; to express their attitudes, feelings and thinking on these experiences in the actual situations in which they occur, in the face of opposition and learning they have little to fear from this vociferous opposition to oppressive or repressive attitudes in other people.

PURPOSIVE CONDITIONING

Purposive conditioning is such as is effected by the purpose behind our activity. We are conditioned by external reality according to the purposes of our activity. Thus if purposes, conscious or unconscious, behind our activity change we will experience different facts of conditioning. This is readily seen with regard to two types of purpose, Revolutionary Purpose or Activity directed towards the creation of social change and Conservative Purpose or activity directed towards the maintenance of the status quo.

INSTRUMENTAL CONDITIONING

Instrumental conditioning is such as results from the success or failure of our endeavours. Successful activity tends to be strengthened and unsuccessful activity tends to be weakened by the effects of satisfaction or frustration as the case may be.

(c) MEDITATION

Meditation in its varied aspects has been called the greatest of pleasures by the great philosophers. Meditation is:

(a) The mental process of systematic reflection on any particular subject or thinking.

(b) Dreaming and exercising the imagination and intuition while awake.

(c) Waking consciousness devoid of thought or the condition of 'No Mind'.

It seems absurd to describe meditation as 'thinking' and 'thoughtlessness' at the same time, but the range of mental states covered by the word have quite varied and distinct meanings. There are three major areas related to the term:

(1) Buddhist meditation - (2) Yoga meditation

(3) Meditation as systematic reflection practised by the Ancient Greek Philosophers.

Every day you should ensure that you have at least half an hour to yourself with nothing to do. Use this period in meditation.

First reflect on your day and think out particular problems you faced or are facing and resolve to tackle them in such ways as your are now thinking out. Next spend fifteen minutes doing the following exercises:-

(1) Relaxation and Removal of Tension.

    (a)   Recline in a comfortable position.

    (b)   Concentrate on the sensational and physical aspect of consciousness, relaxing the muscles of the body in succession until you have acquired a state of body relaxation.

    (c)   Let your breathing be slow, regular and deep.

    (d)   Let your mind wander to relaxing and soothing memories or imagine yourself in stable and pleasant circumstances and environment.

    (e)   The stages of contemplation you now should go through are joy and pleasure accompanied by thinking or dreaming; well being; neither joy nor pleasure and no mind or thoughtlessness. Having been in a state of 'non-thinking' for a few minutes thought will return but may be suppressed and particularly easily with practice.

    (f)   Visualise or project images of yourself; develop a positive and objective self image.

(2)   Whenever worried about anything; having identified what it is that is worrying you, postpone thinking about it for 24 hours and engage in some remote and unrelated pleasurable activity. 'Escape' in other words.

(3)   Learn to control and avoid emotions which produce negative feelings or destroy your feeling of wellbeing. This can be done by focussing the attention on unrelated objects or by considering those feelings as unobjective and unnecessary. Ascertain the causes of such feelings and avoid or dominate the producer of such feelings.

(4)   Train and control your attention by (a) voluntarily concentrating on objects and (b) shifting and focussing the attention on one object after another.

(5)   Learn to identify causeless depression or pessimistic moods and project oneself into any rewarding or pleasurable activity as a way out of them. Learn something!

(6)   Examine yourself for excuses regarding your own activity and behaviour and resolve to reform.

(7)   Set yourself a goal which employs your abilities and talents and gives pleasure and satisfaction in its pursuit.

(8)   Project yourself into definite tasks and activities related to your self image and goals.

People who engage in Callisthenics and Yoga and proceed with the range of mental exercises described under Meditation will attain to Samedi or Nirvana or a state of consciousness which is a high level of psychic integration and wellbeing and union with what is the natural and better humanity. If you assimilate and practice what is contianed in this book you will attain a level of general confident wellbeing and find yourself achieving your goals and finding a great measure of happiness.

MANTRA AND MANDALA

Of assistance in Yoga meditation is a word constantly repeated in one's mind and with one's voice eg., 'Om' or 'The All'. This word is termed a Mantra.

A Mandala is an object or symbol on which the vision is focussed while meditating.

If one simultaneously focusses on a Mandala and repeats a Mantra to oneself one will eventually attain a state of 'self hypnosis'.

CONFIDENCE AND SPONTANEITY:

Confidence is unconscious insight into ourselves, others and social situations. It is unconscious faith in our own adequacy. All challenges to confidence deserve to be dismissed whereas a challenge to our abilities or talents will justifiably be met.

Confidence does not describe our limits to ourselves, it describes only what we know unconsciously or consciously that we can do with certainty. It leaves greater possibilities open!

We cannot ever fully know ourselves but we must at all times BE ourselves. We cannot be otherwise than spontaneous. Hesitancy, is itself spontaneous. Spontaneity does not imply the absence of conscious deliberation or for that matter subconscious deliberation. Spontaneity contains either the conscious deliberation of immediate reflection or subconscious deliberation or both together; precipitating responses which though correct are not wholly consciously analysed.

THE SELF IMAGE:

In situations we may be held back by 'self consciousness' and hesitate in acting or participating. What is happening here is that we are trying to visualise ourselves and other peoples repsonses to us in specific roles or activities. This 'visualisation' is entirely a waste of time and hinders our action and development; unless we accurately visualise and project our visualisation; both of which hinder our action and prevent us from unseflconscious participation. The eye sees, yet cannot see itself! We are unconsciously ourselves when we realise that in all situations we can only be ourselves, that we can never see ourselves as even one other individual sees us, that objective and mature as our 'self image' may be it can never be fully accurate and that we are subject to change and development in wide areas of the personality. The objective must be, to be of original and unselfconscious mind and personality which is attained by 'self forgetting' and doing whatever you will. The Mind can think yet cannot think itself. The sword can cut yet cannot cut itself. Ego is ultimately unknowable.

V : CONSCIOUSNESS AND MIND CONTROL:

There are two aspects to consciousness; sensory and physical consciousness and thought. Mind control is, the action of directing ones attention in the realm of either sensory or mental consciousness.

Attention to aspects of mental consciousness, to thinking and imagination distracts us from attention to sensory consciousness and vice-versa. If we wish to stop thinking about a subject which is the cause of worry or which is causing undesired emotional response within, then it is only necessary to focus ones attention on the variety of aspects of sensory consciousness, visual, auditory, and the like. By learning to focus our attention according to our desires or will, we can be very effective in shutting out emotionally disturbing or unbalancing aspects of impressed or subjectively generated consciousness.

LEVELS OF CONSCIOUSNESS

The levels of consciousness generally experienced are those of Strong Emotion and Excitation, Alert Attentiveness, Relaxed Wakefulness, Drowsiness and Sleep.

The first of these is evidenced by poor lack of control, disorganisation of responses or freezing up, which results in cases of rage or terror or other stong emotion.

Awareness in this state is diffuse and confused and the attention divided. An electro-encephalogram registers desynchronised low to moderate amplitude waveforms of fast mixed frequencies in this condition.

Such extreme situations of emotional upset must be avoided whenever possible; they often result as a consequence of bottling up fears or hatred over a long period and having the dam burst by a triggering indcident. However, the control and direction of ones attention and 'keeping ones head' are essential to avoiding such experiences; they inevitably imply the surrender of the will to sensuous and imagined realities.

Alert attentiveness is accompanied by effieient, selective responses and quick reactions organised for serial patterns of response. Attention is selective and may vary or shift, we experience what is generally called concentration, tend to anticipate developments in our situation and have a definite 'mental set'. An electro-encephalogram registers 'Beta waves' or partially syncronised mainly fast low amplitude waves.

Relaxed wakefulness encompasses routine reactions and creative thought. Attention wanders, is not forced and favours free association. Relaxed wakefulness is characterised by an optimal 'Alpha Rhythm' of synchronised waves of frequency about 14 cycles per second whereas 'Beta waves' have frquencies of about 17 cycles per second.

'Alpha Waves' co-exist with a state of creative meditation whereas 'Beta Waves' co-exist with a state of attentive concentration.

In solving mathematical problems of a routine nature one would be 'in Beta', in writing poetry one would be 'in Alpha'.

These two states characterised by Alpha and Beta wavelengths are the two states most important for the functions of the minds intellectual capacities. In Beta, if we are right handed, the left hemisphere of the brain is more active than the right and 'in Alpha' the right hemisphere is more active than the left. The two conditions may be respectively associated with Analytical and Holistic processes.

It is possible for the individual to train themselves to induce either the Alpha or Beta state of consciousness. The methods of Buddist and Yoga meditation are aimed at attaining the Alpha state and liberating the creative powers of the intellect. A method is to place oneself alone in a relaxed position and using a 'Mantra', a meaningless sound for example 'OM' repeatedly or by staring at a fixed object or 'Mandala', to succumb to the generated Alpha rhythm.

General seclusion in wakefulness alone, combined with free association will usually bring about of itself the Alpha condition. To get from the Alpha to Beta condition one should concentrate one's attention for a time on the sensory and physical aspects of consciousness and preferably take physical activity requiring the use of hand, eye and brain in co-ordination.

The other states of consciousness are drowsiness and sleep. In drowsiness there is reduced Alpha low amplitude waves and one enters dream-like states of imagery and reverie, generally known as 'day dreaming'. These 'day dreams' are conducive to healthy intellectual activity and creation as are any of the aforementioned states of consciousness. They allow what is in the subconscious mind to surface, often giving us personal insights of great importance.

VI : JAPAM:

Japam is the process of endlessly repeating a maxim or aphorism to ourselves; to the point where it sinks fully into our subconscious and consequently is an unconscious determinant of our behaviour. It is similar to prayer but does not have any divine object and is not an act of adoration. If for instance we repeatedly invoke the phrase 'I will be courageous and confident' it will eventually have effect on our attitudes and behaviour and we will indeed become courageous and confident.

If we look at our short comings and psychological weaknesses and invent similar phrases, make a collection of these phrases and repeat them like prayers to ourselves every night before we go asleep, they will transform our lives.

So if all else fails, practice Japam.

Helpful JAPAM Phrases:

1. I shall achieve the satisfaction of all my natural needs.

2. I shall achieve all things ordinarily necessary and possible.

3. I shall ahcieve self realisation, self mastery and self manifestation.

4. I will have courage, confidence, kindness, liberality, prudence, temperance, justice and loyalty.

5. I will be high minded, broad minded, free minded and strong minded.

6. I will have right association, occupation, speech, thought, aspiration and mindfulness.

7. I shall not fear the expression of thought or feeling or physical violence and death.

8. I shall not fear peoples envy, jealousy, anger, hatred, disdain or disapproval.

9. I will not cause undue suffering.

10. The causes of failure are ignorance, stupidity and vanity.

11. I will find love, happiness, security and social esteem.

12. OMNIPOTENT AND UNFATHOMABLE POWER IMMANENT IN THE UNIVERSE AND PRESENT AT THE CORE OF MY BEING: GRANT ME COURAGE, STRENGTH AND WISDOM.

13. I will achieve unity and harmony of psyche, sense and soma.

VII : SELF MASTERY:

Self mastery is the conscious direction and control of our energies to the achievement of our goals

There are three aspects to Self Mastery.

Physiological, emotional and mental discipline.

Physiological discipline requires the regulation of nutrition, rest, physical exercise and sexual activity.

Emotional discipline requires effecting a consonance and unity of thought and emotion resulting in rational harmony. A most obvious consonance is that of loving the good and hating evil.

Mental Discipline is the discipline of study, meditation, reflection and problem solving; the exercising of mental ability; the intellectual disciplines of Logic and Mathematics as examples.

THE DESIRABLE IS ATTAINABLE.

DESIRABLE ARE VARIETY OF LIFE, CREATIVE AND HAPPY OCCUPATION, LOVE, PLEASURE AND ENJOYMENT.

ASPIRE TO THE SATISFACTION OF NATURAL NEEDS, PHYSIOLOGICAL, EMOTIONAL AND PSYCHOLOGICAL; THE FULL REALISATION AND MANIFESTATION OF YOURSELF.

WEALTH, POWER OR FAME ARE NOT TO BE SOUGHT FOR THEMSELVES AND ARE JOYLESS IF ATTAINED AT THE EXPENSE OF HEALTH AND HAPPINESS.

ACT, DO, BE; ONLY WHAT IS NECESSARY OR WHAT YOU WILL.

It is immeasurably, more important for our sanity and happiness, to effect control, expression and harmony of our feelings, than it is to be pre-occupied in mental speculation as to meanings, motives and reasons or objective knowledge such as is inapplicable to our immediate life situation.

HUMAN NATURE

Human needs define human nature and determine human activity.

Needs are physiological, emotional and psychological.

These hierarchic needs in their interplay determine behaviour.

In given conditions either the psychological, emotional or physiological needs maybe dominant, but the basic needs take priority in the necessity of their being satisfied and only when physiological needs are satisfied does the requirement for satisfying emotional and psychological needs become apparent.

The hierarchy of human needs may be restated as physiological needs, needs for physical and emotional security, needs for love and affection, status and power needs and need for self actualisation.

Minimum satisfaction of material needs, that is those necessary for the maintenance of health is an essential precondition for the satisfaction of higher needs, sexual, emotional and intellectual.

Given satisfaction of material needs, the relative dominance of the emotional, sexual and intellectual operates consistent with the nature of the individual.

If material needs determine the possibility of the satisfaction of higher needs, then higher needs also determine the possibility of satisfaction of lower needs.

Needs form a complex and integrated hierarchy.

The individual aiming at the satisfaction of the higher needs realises the necessity of satisfying the lower needs as a precondition for the satisfaction of the higher needs, yet may sacrifice the satisfaction of lower needs in the short term for the short term satisfaction of higher needs.

Those who have innate capacities have corresponding needs.

Those of greatest capacity have greatest responsibility.

Humans are mentally, emotionally and physically unique and unequal.

Human differences are small in relation to qualities and needs held in common. Physical needs and appetites vary little.

Variation in the intellect is of the greatest degree of physical, emotional and mental variations.

We are relatively isolated though rarely absolutely.

Complete self-expression is only possible through love relationship with the opposite sex, which union is sexual, emotional and intellectual.

Essential to all normal human relationships are freedom of association and mutual consent or the absence of coercion.

All true human relationships of a positive or rewarding nature are voluntary.

Beauty is never a mere appearance.

Beauty is more objective than sexual attraction is subjective.

All beauty is virtue and all virtue is ultimately beautiful.

Sexual attraction and beauty, though distinguishable, are inseparable; One or the other aspect or neither being dominant.

They who do not love beauty do not love at all.

Virtue is its own defence and it's own reward.

All superiority is ultimately moral superiority.

Never measure your success by the failure of others.

Life is all there is, live for life.

Health requires right aspiration, right association and right occupation.

Right aspiration is the pursuit of Truth, Justice, Beauty and Freedom; Harmony within oneself, with Humanity, Society and Nature.

Right association is the choosing of friends for their individual human and moral virtues and affection.

Right occupation is the condition of earning one's livelihood by honest means and in a capacity suitable to our abilities and inclinations.

Be neither pessimistic nor optimistic but 'Objective-Minded'.

Be neither Epicurean nor Stoic.

Strength of Mind bestows self control.

ACTION:-

Consistency of action requires correct planning, economy and organisation of time and effort resultant in desirable consequence for the actor, through volition, fixity of purpose or will.

We are all born dying.

After death we exist only in our offspring and in our works.

It is the depth and duration of thought and feeling that makes the great.

Behind every great person is a great love and a great hate.

Love of Truth, Justice, Beauty, Virtue and Freedom implys hatred of their opposites.

Love of Humanity is hatred of inhumanity.

Good is the free, harmonious and full development of the individual in life; the complete intellectual, emotional, sexual and physical fulfilment of the human person.

Ugliness is ultimately vice and all vice ugliness.

We do not lose our identity in the service of Humanity; but rather realise it through the service of Humanity.

The recognition of that which is beautiful just and true in others is the recognition of those virtues in ourselves and their demonstration.

The support of others virtue is the support of our own virtue and its converse their mutual destruction.

Hatred of our own faults and those of others is love of virtue and the essential motivation for self improvement.

Criticism of fault is the construction of virtue.

The civilised sympathise with that which is beautiful in Humanity, particularly in the individual transcendence of difficulty and adversity.

An absolute love or hatred of another human being is blindness.

Make the right enemies and you'll make true friends.

The great are those whose work has general appreciation, significance for humanity and acceptance.

The great cry twice in their lives¦once for themselves and once for humanity.

Genius is a perfectly natural aberration from the normal.

The wise seek anonymity, freedom and fulfilment in life.

What people have in common is far greater than their individual differences.

People need people of like qualities to themselves.

The nature of Man is essentially good except insofar as He is deprived of the means to satisfy His needs; in which case He has a tendency to evil or the attainment of His needs by any means and at the expense of anyone.

All natural desires are good; but the deprivation of the means to satisfy one's needs leads to the perversion, displacement or sublimation of one's desires; all of which is unhealthy and forms the basis of immoral and immoderate inclination.

THE LOVE RELATIONSHIP.

The love relationship exists for its own sake, that is, the mutual satisfaction of intellectual, emotional and sexual needs. It exists only for the good of both partners. It is a wholly voluntary and self sustaining relationship. It is not subject to psychological, social or economic coercion.

There is mutual responsibility for all consequences of the relationship. It excludes all others from such relationship with either partner as it is based on mutual preference of both partners for each other; for its duration. Love of anyone to the exclusion of all others or the exclusion of morality is a barbarism.

The experience of love is greater than the fantasy of love.

Desire and Affection, Lust and Tenderness are all natural and right in their place, but they are not Love.

Love is an integration of spiritual, rational, emotional, sensual and erotic or sexual aspects.

Love is a pulse of the Heart and a movement of the Mind.

Love is a feeling of joy and a sense of beauty and wonder.

Love is to will what is good for another.

Those who love take mutual responsibility for its consequences for each other, for love is just and sincere.

Support neither polygamy nor polyandry. Support neither endogamy nor exogamy. Support neither Patriarchy nor Matriarchy.

Man and Woman must be true to each other and themselves both.

Mans liberation is inseparable from womans liberation and vice versa.

The function of matrimony is the support of offspring in a 'private property' society.

The existence of free love is coincident with individual and collective parental responsibility; the absence of reactionary ideologies the necessity of which implies the social necessity of communism, such relationships formed the basis of the original commune. Free love results in an absence of unwanted children, it affirms the requirement of mutual consent of love partners. What love hath joined together let no one else separate. .

To make sexual love with a person for whom one has no genuine attraction or desire , lust or affection is to go against one's nature and violate a fundamental morality.

Happiness is the satisfaction of all natural moral desires and the absence of immoral desire and inclination.

Virtue is Happiness.

The entire absence of desire is death.

Eugenics is:

The science of the reproduction of such humans as results in a continuous improvement of the species.

The mating of individuals of opposite sex as are equal in terms of Genotype and Phenotype;

Innate and crystallised qualities and attributes.

Free, mutual uncoerced selection by the sexes, given facility and necessary opportunity are it's essential pre-requisite.

Only such relationships as are purely voluntary and natural and result from the foregoing, engender such characteristics are are desirable in the species.

Whom love has drawn together let on-one separate.

Whom enmity has placed apart let no-one force together.

GENERAL ASPECTS OF HUMAN NATURE

1.   The human person is ultimately but a slave of their body and their nature.

1.1.   To break this bondage is to sleep or die.

1.2.   The Nature of the human individual is amoral.

1.3.   The fundamental aim of the individual is the pursuit of pleasure and the avoidance of pain in so far as their needs are thus satisfied.

1.4.   The range of human pleasure in living is encompassed by

    (a) The satisfaction of bodily requirements.

    (b) The satisfaction inherent in emotional pleasure.

    (c) The satisfaction of mental exercise, whether thinking or meditating or dreaming.

    (d) The joy that results in harmony of (a), (b) and (c).

    (e) The joys of pure love consumate in sexual union.

    (f) The pleasure of the participative humanities and artistic expression; music, song and dance; painting and writing.

(g)   Scientific discovery or engineering.

1.5.   In so far as the individual has natural and full
satisfaction of their pleasure potentiality they
are virtuous and good.

1.6.   In so far as one does not attain or actualise the
satisfaction of one's natural inclinations or to
the extent that one's natural desires are
repressed, suppressed, sublimed, distorted or
perverted; one automatically leaves the path
of virtue and takes the path of evil.

1.7.   The selfish individual or they who seek their
satisfactions at the expense of others, are the
most unwise and are incapable of genuine self love
and the consequent satisfaction of innate or
natural needs; because of their blindness.

1.8.   The oppression and exertion of unnecessary
control over the individual, whether by themselves
or others has inevitable concommitants described
variously as delinquency, defiance, alienation and
anomie.

1.9.   The resolution of conflict existing between
super-ego and Id, through egotistic rationalism,
powered by libido is an imperative for sanity.

1.10.   Rationality is a harmonious unity of thought and
affective response.

1.11.   To simultaneously discriminate with the Senses,
Psyche and Soma as they act in unison is to be at
ones highest level of psychological integrity.

1.12.   Non-dualism and unity of mental, emotional and
         physical; the psychosomatic or subjective
         consciousness as a whole, is both to know and
         understand both consciously and unconsciously, the
         unity and identity or the disunity and conflict of
         opposites, whether sensations, thoughts or
         feelings.

1.13.   We can never fully understand ourselves; yet we
         always are and always know ourselves.
         Consciousness is everything known to the
         individual at one time.

1.14.   Emotions:

         Cardinal Emotions are:

    (1).   Love and Hate.

    (2).   Fear and Anger.

    (3).   Joy and Sorrow.

    (4).   Envy and Jealousy.

    (5).   Pride and Humility.

 (1).   Love and Hate:

    (a).   It is essential to love the opposite of what
            we hate and vice versa. Thus love of Truth,
            Justice, Freedom and Virtue is hatred of their
            opposites.

    (b).   We may love or hate; neither love nor hate or
            both love and hate simultaneously.

(c).   The generalisation of love or hate with regard to its objects is the greatest unwisdom of the heart; we must love and hate discriminately.

(d).   To love and hate unwisely is to be benighted.

(e).   To love and hate indiscriminately is to have no self control.

(f).. To love and hate spontaneously is to be natural.

2.   Fear and Anger:

(a).   We can be angry at what makes us fearful and fearful of what makes us angry. We can be both fearful and angry or neither fearful nor angry.

(b).   Fear and Anger, either may change into the other.

(c).   Righteous anger and objective fear are both good as they effect rational action as does love and hatred.

(d).   Fear based on ignorance and superstition is the greatest unfreedom.

3.   Joy and Sorrow:

(a).   Joy and Sorrow are the essential sthenic and asthenic respectively.

(b).   We may experience joy, joyful sorrow or sorrowful joy or sorrow.

(c).   We may know joy or sorrow or neither joy nor sorrow.

4.   Envy and Jealousy:

(a).   Envy is a non-malevolent feeling we experience at the good fortune, qualities or possessions of any other individual which we ourselves would like to have.

(b).   Jealousy is a malevolent feeling directed against one who unjustifiably acquires or attains that to which we have justifiable claim or against one whose aims are the unjustifiable attainment of what is ours by natural right.

(c).   Jealousy is a consequence of the deprivation or intended deprivation by one of another; the latter having justifiable claim, in their own eyes, to that of which they would not be deprived and which the other seeks to or has deprived them of.

5.   Pride and Humility:

Be neither Vain nor Humble; but proud of our Virtue. Emotion is that which constitutes the interaction of Mind and Body, underwrites their potential or actual harmony or disharmony and integrates, Sense, Psyche and Soma. In the exercise of emotions in extreme; Catharsis is the ultimate resolution of conflict existing between Id and Super-Ego.

The dialectic resolution of thought results in a dialectic resolution of emotion and vice versa.

Opposite emotions tend to inhibit or neutralise each other.

1.15. Human Motivations Are.

(a) Feelings or Emotions in so far as they require satisfaction and are a determinant of activity.

(b) The attainment of pleasure and the avoidance of pain.

(c) Aggression and Security needs.

(d) Sexual gratification.

(e) Self preservation.

(f) Power and Status.

(g) Material Gain.

(h) Love and Affection.

(i) Freedom of Body and Mind.

(j) Recognition and Self Expression.

(k) Self Actualisation.

(l) Desire for Immortality.

These basic motivations are inherent in every individual; and to greater or lesser extent any one of them may be dominant, they can form different hierarchies of importance to an individual in particular circumstances.

1.16. Human Virtues.

These comprise the following:

    (a) Prudence.

    (b) Fortitude.

    (c) Temperance.

    (d) Justice.

    (e) Kindness.

    (f) Courage.

    (g) Liberality.

    (h) Honesty and Truthfulness.

    (i) Loyalty.

Only the virtuous can see virtue.

Only the vicious truly know vice.

1.17   Nothing matters except that we continue to live and not
suffer; to have physical comfort and freedom of the
person; to have freedom of thought, speech and moral
activity. To enjoy, to live, to be happy is all.
Ambition is vain and love and humanity are the greatest
riches.

One should aim only at achieving that which is necessary
for our wellbeing and happiness or is to our natural
inclination of mind, temperament and body.

1.18. Conditioning.

> (a) Conditioning is or can be affective only through
>   operation of circumstance whether natural
>   artificial or contrived, through the modification
>   of drives and emotions.
>
> (b) Ultimately; logical or philosophical man will act
>   ᴬ volitionally and in the face of or in line with
>   such factors as conditioning drives or affective
>   responses.
>
> (c) Ultimately the Mind, the Ego, the 'I' is incapable
>   of being conditioned, it is at all times detached
>   whether conscious or unconscious of its operation;
>   sensory, psychological, psychic or rational.
>
> (d) 'Psychological Man' and 'Philosophical Man' are
>   inseparable; the psychological and the logical, as
>   existent and expended in feeling, emotion and
>   thought form a natural and indivisible unity in and
>   of the rational individual.

Work; that is, purposive creative activity, sensory, mental and
physical, is essential to the health of the individual.

Moderate exercise on an ongoing basis of the whole capability
and capacity of the individual; faculties being exercised and
expressed in rhythmic harmony is of paramount significance to
the wellbeing of anyone.

One is what one is born and what one makes of oneself.

The only possibility of creation of a better future lies in the
reproduction, education and culture of the superior or best
individuals and the exclusion of the reproduction of
inferiority. By 'inferior' or 'superior' I refer solely to
genotype.

Philogenetic and Ontogenetic aspects of human evolution are
inseparable.

Genius is a perfectly natural aberration from the normal.

The essence of the individual is what they are born or are
innately.   Interaction with nature and social intercourse
together constitute the condition of the development of the
individual.

Intelligence is ultimately moral and all morality ultimately
intelligent.

Scientifically superior society is materially and morally
superior.

All superiority is ultimately moral superiority.

The individual who does not love common Humanity is a friend to
knowone.

1.19.   There are four main aspects to the individual psyche.

They are Will, Intellect, Emotion and Sensation.

The emotions are the interface of the mentality and
sensational aspects of consciousness. All thoughts have
an affective component. All emotion has a physiological
basis. Emotion is experienced as a part of
consciousness which is both mental and physiological.

Intellect has the aspects of Logic, Analysis and
Synthesis, Intuition, Imagination and Memory. Memory
underwrites the possibility of mentality.

Sensation is the data impinging on the Ego through the senses; sense consciousness as distinct from mental consciousness.

Sense perception and the images or impressions of the senses form the basis on which mental consciousness develops and exists.

Will is the assertion of self motivation. Common to everyone is the Will to:

(1) Survival and Life.

(2) Sex and Reproduction.

(3) Love and Affection.

(4) Power and Freedom.

(5) Truth and Knowledge.

(6) Fame and Fortune.

The aspects of Will, Intellect, Emotion and Sensation operate in the individual in such a way that any aspect can be relatively dominant in given circumstances and in general.

ASPECTS OF THE PERSON

The nature of the human person may be encompassed three. Mind, Heart and Body; Mentality, Personality and Sexuality. In the naturally healthy person all three aspects operate within a single integration, any of the aspects being dominant depending on situation, intrinsic mood and needs.

These three aspects comprise a unity of psyche, sense and soma, an integration of conscious and subconscious mentality and motivation of a harmonious type. Segregation of people on the basis of sex and class result in the distortion of the three aspects of personality and we find ''atomisation' of the individual in society and the existence of 'emotional plague' and social irrationalism.

The three aspects of the person corresponds with the three aspects of love between the sexes.

Love of Mind or Psyche.

Love of Heart or lovelonging.

Love of Body or sexual attraction.

The aspects of the person can be further differentiated into those of spirituality, rationality, emotionality, sensuality and sexuality.

1. Only desires, reflexes, drives or feelings can be conditioned.

1.1. Only I and I alone can know my own mind and my own psychological state.

1.2. The Ego, that which out of the depths of Mind; unconscious of itself utters 'I', the 'I' that thinks; the Will; this existential 'I' in its utterance both proves and verifies 'Ego' and 'Self'.

1.3. The 'I' is inviolable in life.

The origin of my thought is unconditioned.

The great are great because they endure and suffer for the universal cause.

1.4. I think therefore I am.

I see therefore I am.

I feel therefore I am.

I am whether I see, feel or think or not.

I am, who am.

I, who think and know 'I', both prove and verify my own existence.

I am at the centre of my sensations, thought and feelings; my existential self.

PSYCHOLOGICAL SELF RULE

1.1. The human individual is both a social and a sexual animal.

1.2. The higher human nature may be accurately described as embodying a unity of the Philosophical and Psychological.

1.3. The objective world or Universe of which we generally remain incognisant, underlies all the actualities and possibilities such as dialectic interaction brings into being or causes to be.

1.4. The objective world, the Universe; is reflected in the
totality of human consciousness; sensory, mental and
emotional.

1.5. We remain aware of the rudimentary form and aspects of
the capacity of retention, recognition and recollection.
We also experience and can analyse the significance of
dreams and are aware that many processes of 'mental
incubation' precede subsequent intuitive insights.

1.6. In the face of Nature and Society we grow either in
peace and harmony or in the transcendence and overcoming
of difficulties.

1.7. The individual contains four irrefutable aspects to their
consciousness.

(1) The Id or instinctual wisdom based on the avoidance
of pain and the pleasurable gratification of the
senses and basic drives. This instinct is
genetically transmitted and culturally re-enforced
or effaced.

(2) The SuperEgo or innate conscience genetically
transmitted and culturally and psychically shaped.

(3) The Ego; that which thinks and its internal
reflection of itself; such as is exemplified when
we think 'I'; and the self image respectively.

(4) Libido is life-force and inseparable from sexual
potency and physical vigour. It powers the thought
process and is the source of all energy expended
psychically and sexually.

The Id seeks the avoidance of pain and engages in the search for pleasure. The Libido powers both psychic and sexual human operation. The SuperEgo strives to allow the Id have its way insofar as it does not violate the ethical code which underwrites the SuperEgo.

The Ego is the conscious or unconscious aspect of Mind which integrates SuperEgo and Id and leaves the Id free within the limits to which the Ego has rationalised the SuperEgo and Id.

Any aspect of consciousness; SuperEgo, Id, Ego or Libido may in certain life situations be the dominant aspect of the consciousness and determine behaviour.

1.8.   There are two aspects of brain activity which penetrate our mental consciousness.

They are:

(a) Conscious Mind.

(b) Unconscious or Subconscious Mind.

1.9.   Conscious Mind is the dominance of the Ego.

2.0.   Subconscious or unconscious mind generates spontaneously the basis of stored but unrecalled memories. What is suitable for application in the immediate and contemporary reality becomes conscious and is operated on.

2.1.   The conscious mind is not necessarily dominant with regard to the unconscious mind, yet it is certainly so during thought activity which would fall within the context of logic in its most general or particular aspects.

2.2. If there are unresolved contradictions existing
in our subconscious then there is conflict between
SuperEgo and Id which has not been resolved, the
individual being an ethical or moral "schizophrene."

2.3. The conscious mind may direct and control the
subconscious by auto-suggestion or by the exclusion
of externally generated suggestion or conditioning.

2.4. Resolutions of thought and feeling and their
interaction have inevitably positive consequences for
the individual, their CHARACTER STRUCTURE, absence of
guilt and genital confidence.

2.5. When through the exercise of the Ego we eliminate such
phantasms or wrong notions as have permeated our
subconscious; becoming essentially 'Ego-centric'; we
generate an effacement of subconscious conflict.

2.6. When integrated through the action of the Ego, we have
Id and SuperEgo convergent on moral issues; the power of
the Libido is utilised for positive good and
strengthening of mind, while the Ego will subsequently
and consequently operate at its best.

2.7. We are now left with a residue which is no more or less
than the natural integration and conflict-free
harmonious unity self, of self with good society and
ultimately with the wondrous awesomeness of the
Universe's omnipotence.

2.8. Dominance over and control of immediate situational
reality is a precondition for general success in all
endeavour.

2.9.   Self imposed birth control distinguishes Humanity from
       the animals more than any other single factor.

3.0.   Fearlessness is the absence of ignorance, based on
       objective knowledge and subjective insight.

3.1.   The harmonious integration of Id and SuperEgo through
       egoistic rationalism results in a harmonious
       correspondence of conscious and subconscious mind and
       a unity of psyche, sense and soma.

3.2.   The division of the Mind into the aspects of conscience,
       instinct and rationality innate and common to us all as
       well as asserting the existence of the Subconscious as
       underlying the Conscious , are intuitively brilliant
       and psychologically irrefutable perceptions of Freud.
       That the psychological harmony of the individual is
       inextricably connected with the balanced interaction of
       these aspects of the psyche few of introspective
       experience or acute observation of the behaviour of
       others will doubt.

       Conscious mind consists of Thought, Emotion and Will.

       Subconscious mind is a gathering of knowledge and
       wisdom attained by the conscious mind and stored for
       active use.

       Subconscious mind has a teleology, direction and goal of
       it's own distinct from the conscious will which either
       acts in harmony or in conflict with the conscious will.-
       The Id is a gathering of subconscious instinct related to
       physiological, biological and psychological needs.

COLLECTIVE BEHAVIOUR

1. The collective is more than the mere amalgamation of its constituent individuals or parts.

2. The individual contains elements or aspects not manifest in the collective a whole and vice-versa.

3. A significant degree of co-operation underlies the possibility of collective behaviour.

4. (a) The average or 'normal' behaviour.

     It may be considered the 'mode' of collective behaviour or the stereotyped and conventional manner in which 'most members' of the collective "act out" on a recurrent daily basis.

5. Stereotypical behaviour is a consequence of psychological conditioning of drives, reflexes and originally spontaneous behaviour in a given context or situation.

6. Conventionalism is an attempted pattern of behaviour which is aimed as social acceptance.

7. Unconventionalism is a statement of rejection of the conventional, conformism and all equivalence beliefs. It is and seeks to be the assertion of the individual personality; physical, sexual and social freedom.

8. Alienation is symptomatic of rejection by the individual of ideas of persons, individuals and the nature or structure and organisation of society.

9. Speech and conversation are both essential to mental health; as is social and sexual intercourse.

10. It is impossible to effect real social change without a profound philosophic and psychological insight into reality.

11. The agency or catalyst of social change must know and understand human nature thoroughly and the social effects of psychology.

SOURCES OF HAPPINESS

1. Knowledge of the true good and knowledge of the origins of suffering and happiness.

The attainment of the true good in life is the attainment of happiness. The true good is the best development of the physical, emotional and mental aspects of the person for their own sake and for the sake of the consequences of such development for the person concerned.

Knowledge of the specific causes of suffering or happiness is also essential to the attainment of happiness.

The Causes of Suffering are:

(a) Unfulfilled love longing.

(b) The frustration or perversion of natural or moral desire.

(c) Obsessional and immoral desire.

(d) Fear based on ignorance or belief.

(e) Craving for the unattainable.

(f) Craving for illusory good in ignorance of the true good.

(g) Ignorance of necessity or possibility.

(h) Selfishness and Greed.

(j) Vanity.

(k) Injustice.

(l) Unjustified discontent.

(m) Psychological, social or material insecurity.

(n) An underlying disunity of conscious thought.

Happiness insofar as it is a derivative of activity is a matter of involving oneself in such activity as results in pleasure and happiness or satisfaction.

II.   SELF POSSESSION.

Self possession is the single most imperative precondition for the possibility of individual happiness. Self possession is essentially that condition of mind, conscious and subconscious, whereby the individual remains in all situations truely themselves and refuses to sacrifice any aspect of their individuality to the pursuit of aims or goals which are wholly or partly alien to their original and natural inclinations and desires.

The individuals who "have themselves" and are not in any way subjugated psychologically or socially, to other individuals or society as a whole and who do not chase the dreams of others or aspire to the values of others; but dream for themselves and have an individual system of values rooted in independence of mind and thinking and do not abase themselves socially, may be said to be "self possessed".

III. SELF REALISATION.

Self realisation is important for the attainment of happiness. It is the actualisation of latent and original individual potential without which the person is incapable of attaining their higher nature and being their better selves.

IV. SELF MANIFESTATION.

Self manifestation is the assertion of the self realised individual in social or general activity whereby the attainments of self realisation are not suppressed or sacrificed to the ignorance, stupidity or aggressive behaviour of lesser individuals. For example, the individual should not sacrifice their intelligence, morality or knowledge of the truth in the face of aggression.

V. SELF LOVE

Self love means that one wants and seeks only what is for one's good and rejects what is not in line with this aim. Self love is not selfishness as it does not seek one's own good at the unnecessary expense of others. Self love put's love for oneself above the love for other individuals; society and political or social causes. To love anyone or anything more than oneself is to be in peril. One will sacrifice only for what one loves more than oneself.

For instance, one may love Beauty, Pleasure, Truth, Wisdom or Justice more than oneself and reap unhappiness in their pursuit. One may sacrifice all for the cause of the people and gain only suffering. These things are unwise. The pursuit of Wisdom to the detriment of happiness is unwise. Wisdom without the capacity for action is valueless.

VI. DESIRES

Happiness is to a great extent the satisfaction of natural desires. The satisfaction of natural desire is inextricably linked to the fulfillment of natural need. Natural needs are physiological, emotional and psychological. The satisfaction of desire is pleasure which is generally and ultimately good. We may have the pleasure of satisfying our hunger, thirst or our need for sleep; the need for physical, mental and creative activity; the need to understand or the need for sex and love.

Happiness is the fulfillment of moral desire.

Unhappiness is the frustration or perversion of moral desires.

All desire has a natural end and consequence.

The absence of desire is death of the spirit and the flesh.

Desire for the absence of desire is a 'death wish'.

The acceptance of the impossibility of satisfaction of certain natural desires due to material or social circumstances can help us to attain a degree of contentment; but it falls short of the happiness that the satisfaction of those desires would bring.

The fewer and simpler one's desires the greater one's chances of happiness.

VII.   POWER AND FREEDOM

Individual power and freedom are inextricably linked.   The degree of power we exercise, over Nature or other individuals is often the degree of freedom we possess and conversely the degree of power Nature or other individuals exercise over us is usually the degree of unfreedom we suffer.   Power to implement our wishes through others rather than vice versa generates a degree of happiness and satisfaction.   Around the conflict of power and freedom originates all political thinking and all questions of ethics.   We all have the power over others to certain given physical and social freedoms.   That is we have the "power of freedom" whereas political leaders may have the "freedom of power".   The consequences of the exercise of freedom or power is a matter of social concern and the realm of ethics.   It is generally accepted that individuals should not have power over other individuals except in their own interest or the interest of society and must be answerable to society for the exercise of such power.   It is evident that an employer or the state exercise power over individuals which is often of an unnecessary and anti-social or reactionary character.   The power money exerts over some individuals has to be seen to be believed.   The abuse of power ultimately brings its loss and freedom of thought, speech and expression, person, association, occupation and aspiration and geographic and social mobility are all freedoms underwritten as a right to all members of a morally just society.   They are also essential to the possibility of individual happiness.

VIII. LOVE

Mutual love between the sexes is the greatest happiness in life. It has three aspects; the sexual, emotional and mental and all three aspects are essential for it to endure. We have lust, passion and love, desire and affection, lust and tenderness as essential to all affairs of the heart.

The love of friends of both sexes has components of mentality and personality and is a source of great happiness as does love of brothers and sisters and parents and offspring. These statements are not utopian or fanciful and not to love or not to be loved is a source of great unhappiness.

IX

Happiness is the satisfaction of natural needs and appetites; the fulfillment of natural desire and function.

In virtue lies happiness.

The virtueous individual is the natural individual.

The death of "love longing" is the death of loneliness.

Humanity can never fully understand itself; it can know itself, yet to understand itself it must transcend that which it is; an obvious impossibility.

The rational mind is rooted in wisely discriminate feeling.

The young are unwise only insofar as they are unconscious of their wisdom or lack of it.

Wisdom without the power to act is futile.

The virtueous individual most fears the loss of their virtue.

We all fear loss of Ego control.

Usually, respectful people are self respecting.

The animal adapts to Nature and through this evolutionary adaptation survives. Man not only adapts to Nature but adapts Nature to Himself in the process changing His own nature and evolving; generally surviving at increasing levels of sophistication. If society brings about the adaptation of the individual; the individual also brings about the adaption or change of company and society.

X. POISE

Poise is essential to serenity and is rooted in the intention to do, say and act as one may; irrespective of the consequences for ourselves or the nature of others responses. It is the deliberated manifestation of the desire to "be ourselves" and say or act as we will and deem proper and accept the consequences or control them in our own interest.

XI. THE EGO

The Ego; that in us which thinks; implicitly knows its own existence; the 'I', the intrinsic being that we all are, is no single solitary accident existing in isolation. It is a manifestation of the marvellous power inherent in the Universe, to generate life and view itself through the Human Consciousness it thus creates. It is an individual personality existent consequent of the evolution of the Species.

Behind the existence of the individual psyche lies the power of the Universe itself, the unknowable and unfathomable principle and substance whereby the All is everything it is and we are also, as it's witness and epitome.

XII. PREREQUISITES OF WISDOM

A.   1.   To be of accurate perception.

    2.   To be of good judgement.

    3.   To be capable of sound reasoning with both facts and ideas.

B.   1.   To be capable of controlling emotion.

    2.   To have aesthetic and moral sensibilities.

    3.   To be strong willed.

    4.   To be capable of sustained effort.

    5.   To be strong enough to face reality, honestly and without hypocrisy and delusion.

C.   1.   While being sociable to maintain essential independence of thought and action.

    2.   To recognise the opposite factors of competition and co-operation in humans.

    3.   To claim no more attention than is our due.

4. To produce economic and social value underwriting and justifying our own existence.

5. To be political with regard our own interests or our class interests in society.

D. 1. The pursuit of knowledge for its own sake and for the .sake of its application to effect change or progress.

2. The creation of material, social or aesthetic value.

3. (a) Self knowledge and acceptance.

(b) Understanding of human nature devoid of both romantic illusion or degenerate pessimism.

(c) Self Analysis and Introspection or Meditation.

PAIN AND PLEASURE

Pleasure is generally good and wholesome.

Pain is generally evil and unwholesome.

Pleasure such as negates pleasure is bad.

Pain such as negates pain is good.

The absence of pain or pleasure is neither good nor bad.

Anything solely the cause of pleasure only is good.

Anything solely the cause of pain only is bad.

Anything solely the cause of both pain and pleasure is a mixture of good and bad.

There is no such thing as pleasurable excess, all excess leads to or is painful in itself.

Pleasure and pain also may be physical, emotional or mental.

ONESELF

I am first foremost and totally myself.

If I do not have or possess myself I possess nothing and am at the mercy of all.

I am no more and no less than myself; the totality of what I think, feel, experience and do.

I am the existential "I", a soul; and at the centre of that soul a Will.

I am not a name, number, category, occupation, title, class member or a distinction as such.

I am not a collection of wealth or poverty.

I am a unique person in all respects.

"I" am my greatest possession.

I am at the centre of my being, a Will and should will:-

(a) The satisfaction of all my natural needs and desires.

(b) The complete development of my person; all physical, mental and emotional aspects of personal being.

(c) The attainment of active Self Realisation, Self Expression and Self Manifestation.

(d) The attainment of Wisdom.

(e) The fulfillment of moral purpose in my life.

(f) To be an agent of Truth and Justice.

(g) To attain Success and Happiness.

(h) To create the beautiful and the useful.

(i) To act so as to maximise individual and collective freedom.

(j) To counter reaction and aggression.

(k) To attain the best possible material mode of life and existence.

(l) To be "aimless" and "ungrasping", for having singular or narrow goals in life distracts from objective perception of oneself and social and economic reality and to "grasp" at life is to lose everything.

(m) Not to have unattainable goals which generate discontent.

(n) To act, do and be only what is necessary or what I will.

(o) The meaning of life is to be found in the worthiness of ongoing states of consciousness; the pleasure or happiness they bring or the attainment of self realisation and humanitarian aspirations.

(p) I know myself existentially in the NOW; yet I will never fully understand myself.

Desirable things include the following:

(1) Variety of Life.

(2) Creative and Happy Occupation.

(3) Love and Sex.

(4) Pleasure and Enjoyment.

All are attainable without undue effort.

Wealth, Power or Fame are not to be sought for their own sake and are joyless if attained at the expense of health or happiness.

The person is not what they are merely by relation to other people; they are what they are, essentially; to themselves.

I cannot love others unless I love myself and vice versa.

We love ourselves only if we love the common humanity of which we are a part.

We all have to make an act of faith in ourselves and Humanity.

Any philosophy which debases the value of the individual person is opposed to the common interest of Humanity ultimately.

The individual who puts their personal interest above the common interest is anti-social.

What is important about the person is their intelligence, intentions and affections as expressed in attitudes and actions towards others.   These are altogether or partly moral, amoral or immoral.

Soul is the essence of the individual human.

Soul is also the common humanity.

Soul is the centre of consciousness and subconsciousness both.

Ego; the rational and existential identity of the individual is soul.

The Ego THINKS, FEELS and WILLS.   It is self aware and self interested.   WILL directs our activity to the satisfaction of Desires and the achievement of Goals.   Goals are conscious or subconscious aims in life.   Desires are spontaneous feelings directing our activity to the satisfaction of Psychological, Biological or Physiological needs.   The WILL integrates the personality and determines the extent and kind of our activity.

PROBLEMS OF LIFE

Problems facing the individual in the pursuit of health and happiness are:

(1) The Material Problem. The problem of acquiring life's necessities.

(2) The Social Problem. The problem of social classes, exploitation and injustice. We must overcome, eliminate or endure social injustice where immediate change is impossible. Ultimately collective social and political action combined with science and economy eliminate these problems where they bear on the material problem.

(3) The Problem of Understanding. There is:

    (a) Objective Reality, or the world external to ourselves of which we are a part.

    (b) Subjective Reality or the world of our sensations, thought and feelings.

    (c) The relationship between the Objective and Subjective.

    (d) The relationship of individual psyches.

    (e) The relationship of the individual subjective reality and the collective subjective reality. It is the inter-action of (d) and(e) which generates art and self knowledge and(c) which generates science.

The problem is to know Nature, Society and Humanity (Oneself and Others)

(A) Factual Knowledge

    (1)   Discovery and comprehension of facts.

    (2)   The weighing and comparsion of facts.

    (3)   Predicting hitherto unobserved facts.

    (4)   Consistency of observed facts.

(B) Explanation. The relation and comparsion of ideas and concepts.

    (1)   Theoretical exposition.

    (2)   Coherence and logical consistency.

    (3)   'Clarity' and 'Simplicity'.

(4)   The Problems of Emotion.

The problems of emotion is that of the stable, balanced and appropriate experience, control, response and expression of emotion. To a great extent what we 'perceive' and think determines how and what we feel.

The subconscious processes behind our dispositions of attitude and thought are instrumental in evocation of emotional response.

Cardinal Emotions are:

(A)   Love and Hate.

(B)   Anger and Fear.

(C)   Pride and Humility.

(D)   Envy and Jealousy.

All the above opposite couples tend to balance or cancel each other in operation.

(5)   The Problem of Volition.

(A)   Will is the process of instigation, direction, maintenance and organisation of effort to the accomplishment of goals.

The problem of Volition is in part the problem of Motivation. The individual must WANT to attain particular goals which must be related to the satisfaction of psychological, emotional or physical needs.

(B)   Will is the facility of making rational decisions and adhering to them.

(C)   Will is the ability to do such as is necessary, whether to our inclination or not.

(D)   Will is the able assertion of self interest and inclination in line with objective necessity and possibility.

(E) Will is the ability to submit to self imposed rational discipline or externally imposed discipline of an imperative nature.

(F) Will is ultimately the assertion of Self.

(G) Innate to the human person is the Will to:

   (1) Life and Survival.

   (2) Sex and Reproduction.

   (3) Love and Friendship.

   (4) Power and Freedom.

   (5) The attainment of Truth, Knowledge and Understanding.

   (6) Self realisation and Happiness.

The Will actuates the person to the satisfaction of their material, biological, emotional, social and psychological needs.

   (6) The Problem of Action.

      Action is thought or emotion.

      Action is the expression of thought or emotion.

      Action is speech or gesture.

      Action is physical movement or biological function.

      Action can be any combination of the foregoing.

(a)   Action involves risk and uncertainity.

(b)   Action involves will and emotion.

(c)   Action involves judgement.

(d)   Be Active in the Now!

(7)   The Sexual Problem.

The sexual problem stated is the natural recurrent requirement of the human person for regular sexual copulation if neurosis is to be averted.   Sex is a drive much like hunger or thirst and the frustration of this basic drive leads to problems of mental health.   The sex drive is linked with emotional and psychological needs and is not merely an isolated drive like hunger, yet one often hears the terms 'sexual hunger' or 'sexual starvation'.   The 'problem' of acquiring sexual gratification arises out of the class differentiation of people in society, the segregation of the sexes socially and occupationally and the existence of matrimony and prostitution as corrollaries.   Only a classless and egalitarian society where free love obviates the necessity of matrimony or prostitution as the only possible sexual contact of men and women, can efface the 'sexual problem'.

By and large, such society exists nowhere today in realistic and pragmatic terms.

(8)   Happiness.

A minimum of four things are required for happiness. Healthy biological and sexual functioning; successful social interaction; knowledge such as is necessary for our psychological, social and material security and success in labour activity or work.

Pragmatic Guidelines.

(A) The Ten Hinderances.

In the pursuit of happiness, success and fulfillment
there are ten dispositions of personality that
constitute hinderances; they are:

Vanity, Selfishness, Ill will, Distraction, Doubt,
Worry, Stupidity, Ignorance, Laziness and Fear.

(B) The Origins of Enlightenment.

(1) Empirical investigation of the world.

(2) Reflection and Study.

(3) Discourse and Communication.

(4) The emotional conditions of joy, wonder,
vigour, tranquility and equanimity are
conducive to creative dispositions of
thought and imagination.

(C) The Tenfold Discipline.

(1) Right Aspiration.

Right aspiration is the desire to attain to
the Truth; Beauty, Freedom and Justice in living.

(2) Right Concentration.

Right concentration contains four stages of Meditation:

(a) Thought and Deliberation.

(b) The inner serenity which results from the consequence of Thought and Deliberation but which contains an absence of both and is accompanied by joy and delight.

(c) Equanimity and Wellbeing devoid of joy or sorrow or thought and deliberation.

(d) Mindfulness and Equanimity which is neither Wellbeing nor Suffering, Elation or Dejection, Thought or Deliberation.

(3) Right Mindfulness.

Right mindfulness is the observation of the body, sensations, thoughts and states of mind and emotion so as to discipline both desire and elation or dejection in line with the attainment of peace and contentment or happiness.

(4) Right Vision.

Right vision is to perceive the causes and origins of suffering and the cessation of suffering.

Suffering results from the frustration or
perversion of natural desire, desire originates
within the aspects of conscious existence;
corporeality, sensation and perception, emotion,
thought and intuition. The cessation of the
desires occurs within these aspects and the
control of the origin and cessation of desire,
by the will obviates the possibility of its
frustration or perversion. We also seek the
manifestation of natural desires such as can
find ready gratification and result in pleasure
rather than the pain of frustration.

(5)   Right Purpose.

Right purpose is the renunciation of apparent
good and wrong ambition for real good and right
ambition. To aim at self realisation and
happiness or contentment rather than power,
fame or wealth; to seek love and harmony in
human relationships and to aspire to virtue. To
aim at harmlessness toward good and opposition
toward evil; to seek the ways of peace and
non-violence where possible.

(6)   Right Action.

Not to take life except to preserve one's own.
To reject rape, prostitution and incest. Not
to rob or steal. To be truthful whenever
possible.

(7)   Right Effort.

To exert oneself suitably in life so as not to be lax and fall into unwholesome states of mind or mood.

(8)   Right Speech.

To be truthful; not to engage in futile and vain dispute or gossip.

(9)   Right Association.

To associate only with morally decent individuals and avoid the company of degenerates and criminals.

(10)   Right Occupation.

To earn one's living honestly and in a suitable capacity having regard to one's talents and abilities.

If we live without conscious aims our activity becomes directed by unconscious motivations and our "life's mission" inevitably emerges into consciousness and spontaneously creative activity.

(D)   The Problem of Self and Others.

Most people vascillate between the extremes of

    (a)   Selfishness and Selflessness

    (b)   Self consciousness and Self forgetting.

    (c)   Vanity and Humility.

It is wise to be as often as possible at a point intermediate between these two extremes in which case we have:

    (a)   Self Interest.

    (b)   Self Awareness.

    (c)   Dignity.

Imperative to self confidence is self knowledge which by implication is knowledge of ourselves relative to others and the world in general. Also necessary to self confidence is a degree of self interested ambition that is acceptable to ourselves and others. In order to be self confident we must have faith in our own good intentions and must not be paranoid about subconscious motivations.

Imperative for a degree of self esteem or proper self love is a love of common Humanity and respect for people generally. If we do not like people generally we will find that we dislike ourselves also.

If we distrust ourselves we distrust everyone else and vice versa.

If we demonstrate social feeling, empathy and understanding we will inevitably receive the same in return from other people.

(E) ·   EQUANIMITY

Equanimity is emotional stability or tranquility.

Equanimity is attained through insight into human motivation and behaviour.

Equanimity is attained through moderation or self control of desire and activity.

Equanimity is attained through the perception of the true good; the truly significant and the beautiful.

Equanimity is attained through consciously and unconsciously following the path of the necessary only in relation to natural and social determinants of our activity.

To find equanimity is to find the way.

There are three ways to be right.

One must be right in one's thinking and apprehension of reality.   .

One must be right in one's feeling with regard to realities.

One must be correct in one's actions.

Being correct in one's actions requires that we are right in our thinking and feeling and have the courage or will to implement our thinking and feelings in our actions.

Our physiological; biological and psychological needs generate states of consciousness that induce action towards the satisfaction of those needs.

Thought, emotion and action are each interactive with and generative of each other. All thought and action is coloured with emotion.

Our thoughts, emotions and desires all are a force for their own expression.

Treat your person as existential subject and social object and you will preserve it.

THE FUNDAMENTAL QUESTIONS OF PHILOSOPHY

The relationship of consciousness to Reality or Nature. Otherwise stated:

The relationship of Inner or Internal to Outer or External Being and how they form a unity.

The individual is to themselves a unity or compound of sensory and mental consciousness at the focus or centre of which is the Ego.

The Ego is self aware and cognisant of itself while thinking or while being the passive or "thoughtless" focus of sensation or sensory reality.

The Ego proves and verifies its own existence while thinking "I" or "I am".

The Ego Wills, Thinks, Feels and is at the centre of a correspondence of sensory images and perceptions.

The Ego is comprised of innate intelligence or Nous which organises and relates inner reality or consciousness to outer reality or Nature.

The Unity of objective intelligence, law or principle namely Logos and the subjective individual cognition of Logos otherwise Nous; comprises the Unity of individual subjective consciousness and natural objective reality.

Sensation, delivering an implicit correspondence of the senses and sense perceptions to the Ego, is the interface of the individual Mind with natural reality.

The Ego is capable of cognition and recognition or perception of sensory images out of which mental images or perceptions; the memory of sensory images; evolves and develops.

The Ego is capable of differentiation and integration of mental images and thus concept formation.

All concepts no matter how complex are a compound of simple and irreducible or indestructible simple ideas which have corresponding mental and sensory images.

The Ego is capable of Judgements regarding the nature of sensorily and mentally perceived reality.

The Ego is capable of logical reasoning about concepts formed and judgements made about natural or external reality and also subjective, conscious or internal reality. The author would otherwise be incapable of what he is now doing!

Objective Reality or Outer Being is the direct or indirect object of the Senses and the Mind through the senses.

Because of the implicit correspondence of sensation impinging on us through the senses we ascribe it order, consistency, coherence and simplicity.

Behind the "appearance of things" or sensation, lies the "essence of things" or the objectively given reality.

We know we are capable of knowing and understanding Reality; the unity of subjective and objective being, to an indeterminate and indeterminable limit or degree.

Practice is the test of knowledge and understanding, whether in the realm of immediate Nature, Society or Human Consciousness itself.

Experiment verifys or disproves theory or hypothesis.

If there were no objective Logos or no subjective reflection of it , Nous; everything would be "sensational chaos" and "logically unintelligible" disorder.

Appearance is the manifestation of Essence. Noumenon, the essence of Phenomenon, it's manifestation; is knowable to an indeterminate degree or limit.

Not any Phenomenon is known in it's totality and Noumenon is Absolute Essence or knowledge of that Essence, ultimately but not immediately attainable .

Knowledge is both absolute and relative.

All phenomena are ultimately related and interconnected.

Absolute knowledge is knowlwdge of the limitless and infinite.

Relative knowledge is knowledge of the limited and finite.

Absolute knowledge is knowledge of the Eternal and unchanging.

Relative knowledge is knowledge of the transient and changing.

Subjective existence or individual consciousness is a manifestation of objective existence or individual being. If I did not exist, I could not be conscious. As I am conscious I must exist.

I have material existence, being and consciousness.

The world has material and real existence and being as I do.

Other human beings have material existence , being and consciousness as I do.

The mutual existence , being and consciousness of human beings is communicated between them.

Humanity has a collective, shared sensory and mental consciousness which is capable of being communicated between themselves and capable of being analysed or integrated by themselves.

Every individual or particular fact is an absolute truth.

Every absolute truth is an individual or particular fact.

<u>E.G</u>:

"I exist".

"The Universe exists". "Reality is".

"The Universe is Infinite in Space and Time".

"Out of Nothing, comes Nothing."

Nous is not merely the cognition of Logos; it is the manifestation of Logos, cognising Itself.

Logos is the form of intrinsic Necessity and Possibility in Actuality.

Nous is the reflection of this form in human mental consciousness as valid reasoning.

Nous conforms with Logos.

Nous is Logos apprehending itself.

Logos is objective ideal; Nous subjective ideal.

Logos and Nous form a unity in the existential Ego; which union is based in material Being or Substance.

Logos and Nous are congruent as DIALECTIC.

Dialectic is the union of the Objective and Subjective Ideal based in Material Being.

The Individual Person.

The Form of Motion of Matter that is Thought and Consciousness.

The physical, chemical and biological processes of matter in motion throughout the Universe.

The Absolute is the unfathomable and omnipotent Power immanent in the Universe and present at the core of our being, manifest as Life and Consciousness. the identity of the Knower, the Known and the Unknown. Dialectic is the Absolute. It is personal, yet impersonal and Omnipotent; acting in us and through us.

II   THE RELATIONSHIP OF HUMANITY TO NATURE.

Humanity's origins lie in the Animal World. Humanity's
emergence from this world of dependence on Nature to control
and direction of Nature in it's own interest and it's escape
from bestiality has been a complex and is a little understood
phenomenon. Certain distinguishing factors delineates Mankind
from the Animal World.

(1)   Man is omnivorous as distinct from being simply
       carnivorous or herbivorous. It is thought this fact
       was important in the development of the Human Brain at a
       certain stage of Human Evolution.

(2)   Man early developed an erect gait and the capacity to
       walk and run on two legs.

(3)   Man early became a toolmaking and labouring species
       distinct from a predatory one. With the emergence of
       tools, weapons, agriculture and the domestication of
       other animals to serve Human needs, civilisation found
       it's emergence. Civilisation came into being with the
       elimination of cannibalism and the advent of slavery.
       Man not only domesticated animals, He domesticated Man.

(4)   Society is engendered by the needs of Humanity to
       survive in the face of Nature; for the satisfaction of
       bio-social needs and as an essential economic
       organisation of Human labour power and potential.

(5)   Man is a social being.

(6)   Originating out of the development of the Human Hand necessary for toolmaking and Human Speech as necessary for thought communication we can trace the qualitative superiority of Humanity over the animal world.

(7)   Out of the socio-economic formation implicit in all society, evolves it's politics, law and religious or philosophical development which in turn effects change and development of that said socio-economic formation. Philosophical development combined with experiment, otherwise Science, precedes all real progress of a material economic or socio-political nature.

(8)   Humanity has transcended hunting and cannibalism, slave society and is in the throes of elimination of class society wherein economic development is intrinsically linked with the exploitation of Humans by Humans or the domination of Capital over Labour.

III THE RELATIONSHIP OF THE INDIVIDUAL TO OTHER HUMANITY.

(1)   Society enables a general level of material and economic
      welfare to come into being through social co-operation.
      It also enables differentiation in the level of
      individual satisfaction of material needs through
      competition for relatively scarce resources.

(2)   Co-operation and competition are and will be endemic in
      all society; but it is the interest of Humanity as a
      whole that competition be sublimated to the area of
      psychological rather than material need; material needs
      are approximately equal for all. Psychological and
      social needs however differ considerably. Society has
      advanced to a level that it should be feasible to
      satisfy everyones basic requirements of material and
      economic welfare. Absolute and relative degrees of
      social poverty are a direct and indirect result of
      social injustice and exploitation and the struggle of
      classes and nations for relative supremacy and political.
      dominance.

(3)   Society while it guaratees to all in principle, a degree
      of material and social security, eschews, dominates and
      alienates the individual from society to the degree that
      authoritarian political rule directs and controls the
      individual in society and economic processes against
      their Nature.

(4)   Ethics and Politics, are essentially aimed at the
      solution of the problem of Mankind as social beings,
      gifted of reason and economic power and organised in
      classes, in the interest of collective social mobility
      and individual equity.

(5) Human needs define human   nature   and   determine human
     activity.The nature of Humanity is intrinsically good and
     benevolent in relation to other human beings provided the
     person has the satisfaction of their material, bio-social
     and psychological needs. Where humans are deprived of the
     satisfaction   of   natural   needs or these needs become
     distorted or perverted, the   human   being becomes capable
     of evil as a   means   of   satisfying those needs which are
     frustrated or perverted. Where   people   exploit   other
     people to selfish ends we find the origin   of   all social
     injustice and all social evil. The   manifestation of this
     evil is evident   in   all   society   as   relative material
     deprivation of   the   masses   distinct   from   the   ruling
     classes   and   all   peripheral   social evil and "spin-off"
     such as   crime,   sexual   prostitution   drug   abuse etc.,
     validates this.

(6) Love and Hatred, Anger and Fear, are   respectively
     creative   and   destructive   forces   for   survival in the
     psychological   structure   of   human   personality.   Love
     is to construction and harmony as   Hate is to destruction
     and discord. Hatred is required   for   the destruction and
     elimination of social evil. Love of justice implys hatred
     of injustice. Love of justice is   constructive   of   Just
     Legality wereas Hatred of   injustice   is   required to
     elininate unjust law.

     Relationships of a personal type between individuals   are
     determined by rational, affective and   natural   needs and
     tendencies. Love , social and economic utility and mutual
     satisfaction of personal needs all   enter   into   fruitful
     and enduring human relationships. The   emotional   make-up
     of Man is such as   His   reasoning   powers   delineate Him
     from the animal kingdom   and   bestiality. Injury   to the
     emotions or frustration of bio-social   needs or   material
     deprivation all   cause   moral   regression in   the   human
     individual. To   be   unloved   and   uncared for is extreme
     suffering of a most undisirable painful and

dehumanising nature. To be socially poor or spiritually poor likewise marks the soul. Evil engenders evil in opposition to itself and there is the annihilation of evil by evil. Therefore, Good triumphs. Only evil can destroy evil as only evil engenders evil. Wherefrom came original evil? By evil, I mean not accidental material harm, but material, bio-social or psychological harm resultant of the evil intentions of human beings towards each other.

Some people worship evil believing it to be the true Good!

By the fruits of their actions shall ye know them!

(7)   What is ethical or moral is such as is at the same time in the interest of the individual and collective human good; all things that are harmful to the individual likewise harm society or collective Humanity. All things that benefit society and collective humanity are for the individual good.

(8)   Power and Freedom are intrinsically linked in all society. The more individual power the person can exercise the freer they are. The citizen may have the power of freedom and the politician the freedom of power. Freedom in society means that the individual, both directly or indirectly controls the means for the satisfaction of economic or material, bio-social and psychological needs in a way which is harmless to others and society or is for the benefit of all.

(9)   The primary values of Mankind are Life, Labour and Love as related to knowledge or wisdom. The value of labour is that it sustains life, of love, that through it life is procreated and of knowledge that only knowledge raises Mankind above bestiality and animal existence.

(10)   The dehumanisation of the   people as   occurs in unjust
class societies is such as engenders violence.   Poverty
is a terrible   violence, done unto people   and out of
which criminal violence and revolutionary violence and
terrorism   emerge.   Any significant   degree   of
dehumanisation   of the people is the herald of violent
revolution as   social poverty   is the herald of   all
political revolution.

(11)   Politics   is   essentially   the   art   and science of
resolution   of Human   social conflict   by non-violent
means and   methods. Where this fails, we have violent
revolution, terrorism or war.   Revolution   is   class
war   transforming the   nature of a   society in   it's
entirety   and resulting in new class structures or the
elimination of classes.
Terrorism is of   two forms.   Firstly,   state   or
reactionary terrorism inflicted on the masses or people
and secondly, revolutionary terrorism or the inevitable
response   to   the   former   type   of   terrorism.
War as occurring between nations   results from motives
of political and economic subjugation of any   nation by
any other.

IV THE WORLD IS OVER-RIDDEN WITH FOOLS TRYING TO BE CLEVER, MOST OF THESE PEOPLE ARE CALLED PHILOSOPHERS.

IF A MAN IS RIGHT HIS LIFE WILL BE RIGHT

SOME PEOPLE THINK THAT EVIL IS ESSENTIAL TO ALL SUCCESS.

1. KNOWLEDGE.

The first and foremost question that philosophy asks is "Is knowledge possible"; for on the question of the possibility or impossibility of knowledge rests every other question. If we assert "Knowledge is impossible" we are being paradoxical, for this statement at least implys knowledge of the impossibility of knowledge and hence knowledge in some sense is possible. The statement "Knowledge is attainable" while incapable of being proved cannot be disproved and we must rest content with the idea that some knowledge of some unknown extent is possible. Indeed the assumption underlying all scientific enquiry and our attempts and successes in changing the world is that of the unlimited attainability of knowledge. Can any limit be set to the accumulation of a knowledge of Nature, Society or Humankind. Implicit in all our endeavours and indeed implicit in the assumption of Philosophy is that we can acquire knowledge of the truth. All our endeavours would otherwise prove futile.

II HUMAN CONSCIOUSNESS.

In our pursuit of the question of knowledge we are led to consider the nature of the individual human consciousness, which consciousness is verifiably common to all Humanity through communication. We are also led to the consideration of

the nature of the relationship of human consciousness to
Nature.

As everyone will readily testify our consciousness is both
sensory and mental. Our sensory consciousness gathers images
of the natural world through our senses. Mental consciousness
comes into being when we are actually thinking. The two
processes are distinct yet inseparably related as we can only
think in terms of the images of reality we receive through the
senses. The question arises does sense consciousness
accurately reflect the real world or is it all delusionary.
Secondly, assuming that sense consciousness accurately reflects
the natural world; is it possible to come to real knowledge and
truthfully comprehend this world.

The very fact of the surivival of the human race at it's
current level of ascendancy over Nature leads to the
irrefutable assertion that real knowledge is demonstrably
attainable as we have mastered many of the Laws of Nature and
put them to the service of Humanity. Practice verifys theory.

The existence of scientific knowledge and the ability to
transform Nature and Society accordingly testifies to the fact
that no matter how incomplete our sensory perception of the
world may be, it is generally reliably true and we are thus
able to effect an understanding of Nature through mental
reflection on the data supplied through the senses.

Science would be an impossibility if either our sensory
perceptions were unreliable or our thought processes could not
accurately reflect the objectively existent reality. The
discovery of X-rays, electrical measuring devices and the like
extend our sense perception as for example the optical and
radio telescope or the optical or electron microscope. They
render perceptible what was previously invisible.

We have asserted two things and with good reason:

(1) Sensory consciousness accurately reflects natural reality
     and is generally reliable.

(2) Mental consciousness operating on sensory perceptions is
     capable of truthfully knowing and understanding natural
     reality.

In conclusion, since Humanity originates in Nature and is part
of Nature, the culmination of a long process of material
biological evolution; it is easy for anyone to agree with the
notion that individual human consciousness more or less
accurately reflects natural reality and the human mind has
evolved the capacity to grasp this reality.

III HUMAN RELATIONSHIPS.

What is it that determines the nature and quality of relations
between human individuals? I assert unambiguously that the
determining factor is common human need. Human needs define
human nature and determine human activity. Human needs cannot
be satisfied by the individual living in isolation, they can
only be satisfied through collective action and social
intercourse and participation. The whole area of relationships
between Humankind is permeated with economic, political and
moral considerations. Let us first assert that we can see
human needs fall into a range and a hierarchy of dynamically
interrelated specific areas.

Needs are:

 (1) Material and physiological needs.

 (2) The need for physical and emotional
   security in society.

 (3) The need for love and affection, sex
   and reproduction.

 (4) The need for knowledge and understanding
   of self, society and Nature.

 (5) The need for significance, purpose and
   meaning in one's life.

 (6) The need for equanimity, integrity and
   dignity in society.

 (7) The need for pleasurable and satisfying
   activity and enjoyment.

 (8) Freedom and Power needs.

 (9) Prestige and Status needs.

 (10) The need for challenge.

It will be seen that the above list of human needs form a
hierarchy with the most pressing needs being the more basic
material and security needs and requiring satisfaction before
less basic needs become operative as a determining motivation
of behaviour. Yet all these needs are intrinsically related an

they form a complex and dynamic structure for the individual.
While sometimes more basic needs are sacrificed temporarily to
the satisfaction of less basic ones, generally the more basic
needs require ongoing satisfaction before higher needs operate
as a determinant of human behaviour.

The ongoing satisfaction of individual needs is at the core of
human relationships. To the extent that human relationships
effectively satisfy human needs they remain moral. To the
extent that human relationships frustrate, pervert or sublime
human needs and natural desires springing from them they become
immoral.

There are basically two types of relationship existing between
individuals. There are those which are motivatd by survival
and economic considerations and those which are motivated by
love or affection. There are also two distinct divisions
operating on these factors. They are:

(1) Relationships of oneself to one's own sex.

(2) Relationship of oneself to the opposite sex.

In society the economic relationships existing between
individuals are largely "class relationships". Class
relationships to a great extent determine all our relationships
with other people. Natural relationships of a direct and
spontaneous nature and of an affectionate kind rarely exist
between individuals in class society. Class is the origin of
almost all immorality in society. Where the individual or a
class of individuals seeks differential satisfaction of their
needs at the expense of others or everyone else we have origin
of all social evil.

The exploitation of humans by humans is the implicit law of capitalist or modern class society and is the origin of all social evil. The relationships between man and man and man and woman are all tainted by class factors and considerations of exploitation. The political conservative seek to mask and camouflage these class antagonisms in an effort to perpetuate them whereas the socialists are committed to exposing them and eliminating them in the process of building socialist society. Social feeling and natural harmonious relations between humans suffer as a consequence of class realities and the extremes of wealth and poverty in society. The individual who seeks to exploit me or use me to support their aims at my expense cannot be my brother or sister. The christian law of love becomes in these circumstances inoperable, platonic and romantic love withers and humans face humans over the psychological and physical barricade of a lop-sided and selfish egoism and class antagonism.

IV MEANING AND A SENSE OF PURPOSE IN LIFE.

This question has been given many and varied answers by the great world religions. Our perspective however will be Humanist.
It is true that the satisfaction of natural desires leads to happiness and the frustration or perversion of natural desire is sorrow and suffering. Virtue and self realisation and loving relationship all lead to a sense of meaning and significance in our lives and much happiness. The well springs of life are love, work and knowledge. and they should also govern it. The discovery of scientific laws, philosophical truths; the creation of the useful and the beautiful all lend meaning and significance to our lives. Romantic and platonic

love and parenthood all enhance the meaning of life for anybody and all can find significance in social feeling and public service. Many find their raison d'etre in serving a great cause such as Socialism and the betterment of the material, social and moral conditions of the people. Many find their significance in personal sacrifice for loved ones or the common good of Humanity. Ultimately significance is attained through full realisation of the individuals innate potential. It is important for all to find a relatively endurable degree of personal equanimity, integrity and dignity in society if we are to have any shred of personal happiness. Material and Social conditions dictate the possibility or impossibility of this for all but only relatively so. The person of strong character, wisdom and intelligence can in many difficult situations preserve their dignity, integrity and happiness and have the courage to fight injustice and sacrifice for the common good. Human courage and the will to justice and freedom are as perrenial and powerful as the will to life and love themselves.In a situation where basic material needs are satisfied and one has physical and mental health; it is possible for anyone who is dedicated enough to their own dignity and integrity to find the wisdom to live honourably and decently or to have the courage to fight for human rights. We all seek the good life, the good life being the life of love relationship with fellow men and women; virtue and the realisation of our innate potentials. It is often said that only a few are born gifted but everyone can lead a moral life. This is only half true. The path to the attainment of moral understanding is itself very difficult and the morality prevalent in society cannot rise above the material and social level of the people in that society. The possibility of the moral life does not fully exist for millions of humans. The question for millions is one of simple physical survival. Yet the moral life always remains the happiest possibility and the reason for all progressive struggle.

Further Philosophical Aspects.

I.

Active Mind is observation, perception and cognition of objectively existing Reality or Actuality.

Active Mind initiates concepts and first principles.

Reflective Mind is the unity of Logic and dialectical reasoning operating on Active Mind.

Active And Reflective Mind are integrated or united by the imagination.

Active And Reflective Mind together comprise the existence and unity of sensory and mental consciousness; which consciousness is the experiential individual Self or Ego.

Implicit in the unity of Active and Reflective Mind is Will, which Will is individual, derivative of Universal Will and a component of collective and general human Will.

Human Consciousness has two aspects, sensory and mental consciousness and their unity or interaction.

Sensory consciousness has two aspects; one sensation derivative of the world external to the individual as it impinges on the sense organs and two the experience of bodily sensation and emotion or subjective personal consciousness.

Mental Consciousness is thought.

Thought is intuition, imagination and logical reasoning.

Emotional experience is derivative of sensory experience and thought both and their unity or interaction.

Knowing is experiential consciousness.

Understanding is derivative of experiential consciousness through thought.

Understanding is ultimately tested throught application to the sphere of sensory and experiential consciousness.

Understanding is tested through communication with other individuals.

Science is the non-contradictory unity of the Rational and Empirical.

The human person is an harmonious or discordant Unity of psyche, sense and soma; Will, Intellect and Emotion; Conscious and Subconscious Mind; Id, Ego and Super Ego; Mind, Heart and Body.

The human individual is a bio-social being, conditioned by material, social and political realities.

Material, social and political realities are decisive in development of Will, Intellect and Personality.

Political realities and bio-social being determine the degree of freedom of the individual in society and given levels of material prosperity.

II

There is Logos or objectively existent principle, law or form in Nature and NOUS the reflection of this in human mental consciousness.

There is individual and collective NOUS.

Both individual and collective NOUS are a reflection of LOGOS.

LOGOS and NOUS are congruent as DIALECTIC.

There is objective and subjective TAO.

The unity of objective and subjective TAO is DHARMA.

Implicit in Dialective or Dharma is the unity of:

        (a)   Individual and Collective Will.

        (b)   General Will.

        (c)   Universal or Objective Will.

Karma is the unity of DIALECTIC or DHARMA and action or activity.

Karma is the unity of mental, sensory, emotional and physiological consciousness implicit in being and acting.

Karma is psychosomatic integrity in activity and action.

The individual, general or collective Will are not necessarily in harmony with each other or with the objective or Universal Will.

Dialectic or Dharma consist in the unity of the Personal and Impersonal Absolute; the One, It, The All; manifest as life and consciousness.

The ideal is derivative and secondary to the material; both objectively as sensously perceived or mentally cognised Actuality or Reality and subjectively as contained within the form of motion of matter that is human thought or mental consciousness.

The material has objective existence and delineates the ideal; the existential actuality of which is unknowable and indiscernible.

The concept "circle" while being thought has ideal existence within the thought containing it. What is the nature of its existence?

Both objective Form or the ideal in Nature and Matter imbued with this Form are objectively and subjectively external.

The ideal is implicit in the material; together they form substance.

Matter is tangible and concerete reality, yet the concept or idea of matter is ideal.

The Ideal is derivative and secondary yet inseperable from the Material; being the form of existence of the Material:

    (a) Both as sensuously percieved or mentally cognised.

    (b) Subjectively as the content of mental consciousness or thought, which is itself a form of the motion of matter and material entity both.

Any concept while being thought has existence as the ideal. What is the nature of this existence?

Essence presupposes existence.

Essence and existence are inseparable.

Essence is the actualisation of existence.

All essence is potential or actualised existence.

Essence and existence are ontologically simultaneous.

The actual present contains the potential future.

The actual present is the realisation of past potentiality.

The actual contains the potential and is the result of preceedent potentiality.

Absolute necessity is such that it's negation or elimination is an impossibility.

Relative necessity may be negated or eliminated, increasing the degree of freedom of the individual in Nature or Society.

The potential includes all probability and possibility; excluding only impossibility.

The potential contains all necessity and chance.

What must be, must be; what will be, will be; what maybe, maybe.

There is the Certain and the Impossible. There is the possible.

There is the probable and the improbable, both of which are possible.

There is necessity and chance.

Chance is absolute necessity and necessity is absolute chance.

There is absolute freedom of Will as I can and may Will what I like or as I choose.

The act of willing, itself does not engender or accomplish anything. I can will the impossible though it can never be.

It is action that determines events or the absence of events.

It is political and bio-social interaction that determines potential or actual freedom of the individual.

Action does not necessarily require the Will to Act, action can be spontaneous or involuntary.

Action may be instinctual.

Particular ends can only be accomplished through action based on a recognition of the general truth.

Only action based on the cognition of general truth bestows freedom.

THE ABSOLUTE

The Absolute is the unity , essence and whole of the infinite diversity comprising Ultimate Reality.

It is immanent in and constitutes Nature and the Universe.

It is inseparable from the Universe and Nature.

It attains an identity with the Universe and Nature.

It is manifest in and through Us as Life and Consciousness.

It is omnipotent , infinite and unfathomable.

It is manifest in and through Us as Human Consciousness and Intelligence.

The Absolute is the unfathomable and omnipotent power immanent in the Universe and present at the core of our being; The identity of the Knower , the Known and the Unknown.

The Absolute underwrites the End and Goal of all Existence.

The End and Goal of all Existence is unknowable.

The Absolute contains matter and the infinite extent and myriad forms of it's existence and eternal motion.

The Absolute is the underlying essence and unity of the Matter-Energy and Space-Time continuum we understand the Universe to be.

The Absolute is not wholly definable due to the infinite reducibility of concretely existing matter distributed throughout the infinite Universe.

The Absolute is Ultimate Being, the essence and whole of the objectively existent and infinite Universe.

The Absolute is the unity of the material and ideal that comprises the whole of objective and subjective reality.

'GOD' is the name of the Absolute.

IT

IT is all that is. It is the Absolute.

It is manifest as matter and all the forms of motion of matter; physical, chemical, biological, social and mental.

IT is manifest in and through YOU and I.

The relationship of You and I is a relationship of IT to IT.

The Relationship of I to IT is a relationship of It to IT.

MIND or mental consciousness is a relationship of IT, as You and I, to IT.

IT is the unity of objective and subjective Truth.

IT is Thought, IT is individual and collective Will.

IT is LOGOS; IT is NOUS; IT is BEING.

IT is the ONE: IT is the WAY.

IT is uncreated and infinite .IT is indestructible.

IT is eternal. IT ever has been and ever will be.

IT is all that which is , ever has been and ever will be.

It is the active principle of the Universe, underlying IT's very unity, essence and existence.

'Uncaused' or 'Self Caused' ; IT is the cause of all that is.

Uncreated It creates all. Indestructible IT yet destroys.

It is both creative and destructive.

He and She are the Human manifestations of IT.

The name of IT is the One.

THE ONE

The One is the unity, essence and whole of all that exists.

The One is both objective and subjective and of myriad aspects.

The One is all and is Truth itself.

The One is the Unity of the Absolute and the Relative.

The One is the infinite existent.

The One is both changing and changeless.

The One is unlimited.

The Unity of the many is the One.

The concurrence of opposites is their mutual annihilation in the One.

The One is all that which is and all that which is not.

The One is certain and the One impossible.

The One is Nothing and the One Being.

The One is Material and the One Ideal.

The One is dynamic and the One static.

The One is dark and the One bright.

The One is eternal and uncreated.

The One is neither Good nor Evil but morally neutral.

The Universe forms an identity with and is the manifestation of the One.

The One is both creative and destructive.

The One is ultimately manifest as Matter and the infinite forms of It's motion in Space-Time intrinsic to which is LOGOS or Cosmic Law and Principle.

The One is manifest in and through Us as Life and Consciousness.

The Truth is all and everything that has been is or will be.

Truth regarding the future is purely speculative.

Truth regarding the past is 'Neutral'.

Truth regarding the present is Material in the NOW.

The One is the true Absolute.

The true Absolute is the unity, essence and whole of the infinite diversity comprising the Universe.

The True Absolute is the Soul and Spirit of the Universe.

As Soul the true Absolute is the true nature and whole of the Universe.

As Spirit the true Absolute is the active creative principle of the Universe.

The One is the true Absolute.

'GOD' is the name of the One.

THE WAY

The Way is the path of least action or resistance which effects greatest change in life.

The Way is to consciously or unconsciously follow the laws governing Nature and Human Society.

The Way is to be one with what is Timeless and Eternal and also imperative in the Now.

The Way is the recognition of natural and social reality in our life activity.

The Way is the realisation and manifestation of the true Self.

In Truth and Virtue lie the Way.

The Way is natural and easy.

To seek wisdom is to seek the Way.

To seek happiness is to seek the Way.

To aspire to Justice and Freedom is to seek the Way.

To do all except the immoral is to find the Way.

To love good and hate evil is to know the Way.

To be without fear of the unknown is to know the Way.

To know the Way is to be true to one's nature and destiny.

To be "aimless" and "ungrasping" is to know the Way.

Aspire to Truth and Virtue and you will find the Way.

We are all vagabonds of Destiny.

The Way is neither good nor evil but the path of Virtue.

The way is neither moral nor immoral but is indifferent.

Do not allow conscious goals to dominate your consciousness, rather be "aimless" and realise the unconscious goal or mission of your existence.

Know yourself through knowing others.

Know others through knowing yourself.

Know yourself through losing yourself in unselfconscious activity.

Forget yourself and become involved is social life.

Be yourself in uninhibited expression.

Realise your self in self absorbing creation.

Follow your natural inclinations.

The Way is the recognition of natural, social and moral necessity in our activity.

Humanity engenders It's survival and reproduction through labour.

Labour is action exerted by Humanity in and on Nature and in Society.

Activity; mental, physical, biological and social is essential to health and survival.
Man and Woman are each the complement of each other; they are not intrinsically equal, either mentally, emotionally or physically.

Certain aspects of the human female's nature are superior to those of the human male and certain aspects inferior.

The measure of real freedom we possess is a consequence of rational activity.

Scientific Action Liberates.

Contention and competition are to be avoided except where they are forced on one. There always has to be a loser. Victory is not always a sign of superior humanity.

Harmony and co-operation in society are essential to it's functioning and ultimate human survival.

Creative activity is essential to happiness.

Freedom from desire is essential in order to be able to form an understanding of Humanity and society.

The experience of desire is also essential to the development of understanding.

Involvement and experience of desires and feelings is essential to the possibility of successful action.

To live in the senses is to know unselfconscious ecstacy.

To live in the emotions is to know joy and sorrow.

To live in the mind is to be oblivious of immediate physical, sensory and emotional reality.

Passivity is essential to equanimity in certain circumstances .

Passivity or non-involvement is sometimes essential to survival.

The male is as a mountain. The female is as a valley.

They exist through each other.

The male is active and assertive.

The female is passive and receptive.

Every human person has both male and female characteristics.

On occasion the male characteristic is essential to survival.

On occasion the female characteristic is essential to survival.

The male characteristic is as light and understanding.

The female characteristic is as darkness and mystery.

The male is to the female as The Sun is to the Moon or as Day is to Night.

The male characteristic is virility.

The female characteristic is fertility.

The male characteristic is critical and aggressive.

The female characteristic is considerate and placating.

The male characteristic is courage.

The female characteristic is endurance.

The male is symbolised by the 'Ideal' or 'Form'.

The female is symbolised by the 'Material' or 'Content'.

SPIRITUAL IDEOLOGY

Omnipotent, unfathomable, ineffable Power immanent in the Universe, constituting It's unity , essence and whole; present at the core of my being and manifest in and through me as life and consciousness; grant me freedom of thought,the cognition of moral realism and the courage of rational conviction and scientific faith.

Unify my spirit, intellect, will and emotions as a harmony of personal psyche , sense and soma ; existence and activity.

May my will attain an identity with the Universal and Divine Will and the General Will of Humanity.

May I attain unity with the One and harmony with the Way.

Almighty and eternal God, Spirit and Soul of the Universe, grant me the insight to see the relationship of absolute to relative truth, the changing to the changing , the eternal to the transient.

May I find psychic unity with the true absolute ; Spirit and Soul of the Universe.

Grant me equanimity in the face of insecurity , oppression and injustice.

Give me the strength of right action and the fortitude of enduring wisdom.

Grant me self knowledge and self control ; self realisation and prudent self assertion.

May I attain happiness of mind and contentment of heart.

May I find the Way , the Truth and the Life.

In the name of the One , unity , essence and whole of the Universe , Spirit and Soul of Ultimate Being ;

FOR IT IS ETERNAL AND INFINITE.

THE NINE GREAT HAPPINESSES

The first and greatest happinesss is HAPPINESS OF MIND.
Happiness of mind is rooted in the acknowledgement and attainment of psychic unity with the Absolute or 'God'.
In religious terms it is the "Love Of God".It is unity and harmony with the ONE and the WAY.
A secondary happiness lies in the attainment of wisdom or the cognition of Truth.
The Absolute or 'God' is the unity, essence and whole of ultimate reality .This reality is an eternal unity of the Spiritual and Material.
The Absolute as being the infinite material diversity in eternal motion is impersonal, yet as being manifest in and through us all as Life and Consciousness it is highly personal.
'God' is the Soul and Spirit of the Universe.
As 'soul' 'God' is the essential nature and whole of the Universe.
As 'spirit' 'God' is the active creative principle of the Universe.

The second greatest happiness is HAPPINESS OF THE HEART or the fulfillment of the heart's desires.
Happiness of the heart results from loving and being loved. It is Love Of Humanity.
There is Self Love and the love of others both of which are rooted in each other.
There is sexual love and parenthood, such needs as are satisfied in authentic love relationship with the opposite sex.

The third greatest happiness is creative visual, musical or literary art and investigative science.

The fourth greatest happiness is that of the performing artiste.

The fifth greatest happiness is that of enjoyment.

The sixth greatest happiness is the Cause Of The People or service to Humanity. It is due to the fact that this requires much self abnegation and sacrifice that this happiness is not of the greatest degree. Many find in this happiness a compensation for the absence of the second greatest happiness or the fulfillment of the heart's desires in love.

The seventh greatest happiness is the exercise of political power.

The eight greatest happiness is fame or glory.

The ninth greatest happiness is material wellbeing and security without which life itself or any vestige of happiness would be impossible.

Media Diversity

Economics, Ownership, and the FCC

LEA's COMMUNICATION SERIES

Jennings Bryant / Dolf Zillmann, General Editors

Selected titles in Mass Communication (Alan Rubin, Advisory Editor) include:

Albarran/Arrese • Time and Media Markets

Alexander/Owers/Carveth/Hollifield/Greco • Media Economics: Theory and Practice, Third Edition

Bunker • Critiquing Free Speech: First Amendment Theory and the Challenge of Interdisciplinarity

Compaine/Gomery • Who Owns The Media? Competition and Concentration in the Mass Media Industry, Third Edition

Harris • A Cognitive Psychology of Mass Communication, Third Edition

Moore • Mass Communication Law and Ethics, Second Edition

Palmer/Young • The Faces of Televisual Media: Teaching, Violence, Selling to Children, Second Edition

Russomanno • Speaking Our Minds: Conversations with the People Behind Landmark First Amendment Cases

---

For a complete list of titles in LEA's Communication Series, please contact Lawrence Erlbaum Associates, Publishers at www.erlbaum.com